DESKTOP PUBLISHING

WITH

WordPerfect

Roger C. Parker

DESKTOP DESIGN
S E R I E S

Ventana Press
Chapel Hill, NC

Desktop Publishing with WordPerfect

Library of Congress Cataloging-in-Publication Data

Parker, Roger C.
      Desktop Publishing with WordPerfect.

      (The Ventana press desktop design series)
      Bibliography: p.
      Includes index.
      1. Desktop publishing. 2. WordPerfect (computer program) I. Title. II. series.
Z286.D47P34 1988   686.2′Z   88-50309
ISBN: 0-940087-15-4

Cover design by Holly Russell, Chapel Hill, NC

Cover illustration by Anthony Russo, Providence, RI

Desktop publishing graphics by Beth Domby, TechniProse, Inc., Chapel Hill, NC

Desktop publishing type by Johnna Webb, Pixel Plus, Chapel Hill, NC

Linotronic output by Azalea Typography, Durham, NC

Technical editing by Jane Helwig, Chapel Hill, NC, and Techniprose, Inc., Chapel Hill, NC

Copyediting by Clare Rosen, Chapel Hill, NC

First Edition, First Printing

Printed in the United States of America

Ventana Press, Inc.
P.O. Box 2468
Chapel Hill, NC 27515
919/942-0220

Trademark
Acknowledgments

Ventana Press has made every effort to supply trademark information about the company name, product and services mentioned in this book. Trademarks indicated below were derived from various sources. The publisher cannot attest to the accuracy of this information.

All products are trademarks or registered trademarks of their respective manufacturers.

3M Post-it Notes, 3M CORPORATION
Arts & Letters, COMPUTER SUPPORT CORPORATION
AutoCAD, AUTODESK, INC.
Bitstream, BITSTREAM, INC.
dBase III, ASHTON-TATE
Dr. HALO, MEDIA CYBERNETICS
GEM, GEM Draw, GEM SCAN and GEM Paint, DIGITAL RESEARCH
    INC.
Hercules Ramfont, HERCULES COMPUTERS
HPScanning Gallery, HEWLETT-PACKARD COMPANY
IBM, IBM Selectric, PC, DOS, PC-AT, PC-XT, INTERNATIONAL
    BUSINESS MACHINES
ITC Zapf Dingbats, INTERNATIONAL TYPEFACE CORPORATION
JetScript, QUALITY MICRO SYSTEMS, INC.
LaserJet, LaserJet Plus and DeskJet, HEWLETT-PACKARD
LaserWriter, Macintosh, ImageWriter, Switcher, AppleTalk, APPLE
    COMPUTER, INC.
Linotronic 100 and Linotronic, LINOTYPE COMPANY
Lotus 1-2-3, Lotus Symphony, LOTUS DEVELOPMENT CORPORATION
MacDraw, MacPaint, MacWrite, CLARIS CORPORATION
Microsoft Word, Microsoft Windows, Windows Paint, Excel and MS DOS,
    MICROSOFT CORPORATION
Multimate, MULTIMATE INTERNATIONAL
PageMaker and FreeHand, ALDUS CORPORATION
PC Paint Plus and PC Paintbrush, Z-SOFT, INC.
PostScript and Illustrator, ADOBE SYSTEMS, INC.
Quark Xpress, QUARK, INC.
SuperCalc 4, SORCIM CORPORATION
SuperPaint, SILICON BEACH SOFTWARE
The Clipper, Glue, SmartScrap, SOLUTIONS, INC.
Ventura Publisher, VENTURA SOFTWARE, INC.
WordPerfect, WordPerfect Library and PlanPerfect, WORDPERFECT
    CORPORATION
WordStar, MICROPRO INTERNATIONAL CORPORATION

Author's Acknowledgments

I used to think that Acknowledgments were an empty formality. But, that's not so. *Desktop Publishing with WordPerfect* proves, once again, that books are the result of a team effort. It takes more than an author to bring a book to life. *Desktop Publishing with WordPerfect* simply would not have happened without the encouragement and support of Andy Bangs, Larry Daywitt, Bill Gladstone, William McKinley and—most important—Jeff Sandine.

I'd also like to thank Elizabeth Woodman for her uncanny ability to read between the lines of my manuscript and intuitively understand what I was struggling to say. Hats off, also, to Karen Wysocki who refined my vision of what *Desktop Publishing with WordPerfect* should look like and gave it life.

The real heroes of this book, of course, are my wife, Betsy, and my children—Christopher, Zachary and Ryan—who frequently put up with an absentee husband and father in order to allow me to "write without guilt" till sunrise.

Thanks also to WordPerfect's unparalleled Customer Support Group who always answered my questions with patience, enthusiasm and tact.

The publisher wishes to express appreciation to the following individuals who assisted in the production of this book:

Jeff Acerson
Beth Domby
Rebecca Mortenson
Cheryl Shelly
Johnna Webb
Richard Wilkes

About the Author

Roger C. Parker is owner and president of The Write Word, Inc., an advertising and marketing consulting firm based in Dover, NH. He is the author of *Looking Good in Print: A Guide to Basic Design for Desktop Publishing* (Ventana Press), *The Aldus Guide to Basic Design* (Aldus) and *Using Aldus PageMaker* (Bantam). His clients include Apple Computer, Aldus, Bitstream, Hewlett-Packard, Microrim and Yamaha.

Roger Parker has created and is presenting nationwide seminars on Desktop Design for Promotional Perspectives of Ann Arbor, MI.

The author can be reached at

The Write Word, Inc.
466 Central Avenue, #3
The Morrell Building
Dover, NH 03820
603/742-9673

Contents

Section One: Mastering the Printed Page

Section Two: Design Tips and Tricks

Introduction

With the introduction of WordPerfect's powerful new Version 5.0, word processing will never be the same. While traditional word processing changed the way you organize and generate information, Version 5.0 changes the way you present it by integrating desktop publishing features into its program.

You now can produce professional-looking printed materials.

Compare this: with this:

WordPerfect 5.0 removes the barriers between writing and page layout—the arrangement of copy on a page. Once the domain of graphic artists and designers, the appearance of the printed page is now in your control.

Your documents can feature

- Multiple typefaces, type sizes and type styles.

- Graphic elements such as rules, boxes, reverses and screens.

- Charts, graphs, illustrations and other artwork—even scanned photographs created with other software programs!

Everyone wants their printed materials to be as attractive and persuasive as possible—and WordPerfect's new graphics features are a natural extension of its powerful word processing capabilities.

Why Your Documents Should Look Their Best

Professional-looking printed materials, built around a carefully chosen selection of typefaces and type sizes, are easier to read. Readers grasp your message more quickly and give more credibility to what you say.

In addition, multiple-column documents, which use a variety of type sizes, often are more cost-effective because they accommodate more type, thus require fewer pages. Finally, raw information takes on new meaning and is greatly enhanced when translated into charts and graphs.

Without getting in your way, WordPerfect 5.0 makes it easy to place words on a page as effectively and efficiently as possible, making your printed materials more persuasive, attractive and easy to read.

Who Should Read This Book?

Who will really benefit from these new features? If you create proposals, newsletters, brochures, books, training manuals or other projects where the success of your communications is based on clarity, consistency and readability, WordPerfect can provide the solution to many of your design needs. And *Desktop Publishing with WordPerfect* shows you how to use these features to make your documents look their best.

Enhancing the appearance of your printed materials has never been so easy or so cost-effective. For less than the price of dinner for two, current WordPerfect users can upgrade their software and take advantage of the program's new desktop publishing capabilities.

Veteran and new users may find that WordPerfect's new graphic features eliminate the need to purchase a more expensive desktop publishing program. By integrating page layout capabilities with word processing, WordPerfect eliminates the need to invest time learning a second program in order to enhance the appearance of your documents.

However, if your job involves designing sophisticated, single-page projects, such as posters or complicated magazine advertisements, WordPerfect isn't a substitute for dedicated page layout programs. Art directors and graphic designers may become frustrated by its lack of typographic niceties. In other words, WordPerfect 5.0 offers the capabilities necessary for producing all but the most design-intensive projects.

Version 5.0 is easy to learn. For newcomers, WordPerfect's use of color-coded function keys makes it an easy program to master. Experienced WordPerfect users immediately will find most commands unchanged on the new version, enabling them to use 5.0's enhanced powers with ease. Most function keys operate as before, and **HELP** (F3) is just a keystroke away.

In addition, 5.0 eliminates time-consuming file transfers between word processing and page layout programs when you're designing a document. With 5.0, you can format and design your document while entering text.

In short, WordPerfect 5.0 gives word processing a new respectability. No longer must documents generated via word processing be monotonous in appearance. With its desktop publishing capabilities, WordPerfect-generated documents present a professional image to your clients, customers and readers.

What's Inside

Desktop Publishing with WordPerfect teaches you how to use WordPerfect 5.0 to produce better-looking documents that reflect well on you and your business.

Section One, "Mastering the Printed Page," will help you become acquainted with WordPerfect's new desktop publishing features. You'll learn how to add graphic elements (such as rules, boxes and screens), work with multiple columns and use stylesheets to speed up page formatting. You'll also learn how to integrate illustrations (graphics files) created with other programs, as well as make the most of the various typeface options available with your laser printer.

Section Two, "Design Tips and Tricks," puts the basics you learned in the first section to work, providing numerous examples of basic graphic design skills needed to produce attractive, persuasive documents.

How to Use This Book

If you're not familiar with WordPerfect's desktop publishing features, read Section One carefully, particularly Chapters One through Seven. More advanced users will want to read Chapters Eight and Nine, which cover macros and stylesheets.

If you already know about WordPerfect's graphics capabilities, you may want to review Section One quickly and concentrate on Section Two, which offers invaluable tips and techniques for creating specific types of documents using WordPerfect.

Use this book as a work tool, tagging pages and making notes. You'll want to refer to key passages repeatedly as you encounter similar design challenges with your various projects.

How Well Should You Know WordPerfect?

Desktop Publishing with WordPerfect was written to complement WordPerfect's program documentation, not as a substitute for it. You should already know the basic WordPerfect commands, such as how to

- Enter, delete and move text.
- Print, retrieve and save files.
- Format text, create line spacing, add headers, footers and page numbers.

This book was written with the assumption that your computer and printer are up and running, that you're comfortable with WordPerfect as a word processing program and, finally, that you're ready to forge ahead, learning how to create better-looking documents.

Hardware/Software Requirements

Obviously, you must have a copy of WordPerfect Version 5.0; previous versions don't include desktop publishing features.

In most cases, WordPerfect doesn't require the purchase of additional hardware or software. You don't need to buy an input device like a mouse, for example. Nor do you need an operating environment like Microsoft Windows.

However, WordPerfect's new features may provide the catalyst you need to upgrade your computer and printer. For example, because WordPerfect is a large, multi-disk program—and contains an even more comprehensive spell-checker and thesaurus—you'll find that a hard disk is a near-necessity. If you don't have one, now would be an excellent time to add one, thereby avoiding tedious "floppy-swapping."

Likewise, if you don't have a laser printer, you may want to consider this worthwhile investment. If you already have one, you'll probably find that now is the time to increase the number of fonts (type families) you have available.

Whether you choose font cartridges or downloadable disk-based fonts, the ease with which WordPerfect handles fonts lets you add many new design elements to your documents.

Font cartridges (plug-in circuit boards designed for certain brands of laser printers) contain a specific number of typefaces, type sizes and type styles. They're the easiest and least-expensive way to add visual variety to your publication.

Downloadable fonts—or "soft" fonts—are alphabet and number sets on floppy disks that you transfer to your hard disk. Downloadable fonts offer the most flexibility, giving you a virtually unlimited choice of typefaces, type sizes and type styles. WordPerfect 5.0 has a unique "font-swapping" feature, which preserves printer memory and lets you include up to 250 typefaces, type sizes and type styles on a single page.

WordPerfect's ability to smoothly integrate graphics files may even motivate you to round out your software programs with additional chart, graphics or drawing programs—or even invest in an image scanner.

Because WordPerfect now does so much, you might find it worthwhile to upgrade your monitor and enjoy a clearer on-screen representation of your page layouts.

The money you save because you won't have to buy page layout software may allow you to buy many of these important enhancements that can save time and greatly improve your finished documents. If you're serious about improving the look of your printed materials, I strongly recommend that you invest in the tools that will make your job easier—and less expensive in the long run.

All Aboard

Version 5.0 and *Desktop Publishing with WordPerfect* provide the tools you need to savor the creative design and page layout features of one of the world's most advanced word processing programs.

Eventually, WordPerfect will introduce new, improved versions that will do the job even better—integrating word processing and page layout functions more easily and less expensively. However, don't succumb to the "I'll-wait-for-the-next-train" syndrome. Those who wait will have a harder time catching up than those who are already on board.

By learning WordPerfect's 5.0's desktop publishing features now, you'll be better able to take advantage of future upgrades. While those on the platform are waiting to catch up, you'll be that much farther down the track.

Roger C. Parker
Dover, New Hampshire

SECTION ONE

MASTERING THE PRINTED PAGE

1

Getting Started

Producing professional-looking documents was once a tedious and expensive process, involving many different steps and missed deadlines. Revisions and last-minute changes were costly and often resulted in further delays. And managing all of it could transform you overnight into a candidate for an Excedrin commercial.

WordPerfect's powerful new desktop publishing features offer an inexpensive, streamlined alternative for creating your advertisements, books, brochures, newsletters, reports and training materials as you write them. You now have the power at your fingertips to perform such sophisticated formatting functions as creating multiple columns, choosing from a variety of typefaces, drawing lines and boxes, using graphics and more.

Before you plunge into the details involved in creating camera-ready documents (material you send to the printer) with WordPerfect, let's look at its broad new features and enhancements from previous versions that give WordPerfect its desktop publishing capabilities.

Previewing the Printed Page

WordPerfect's **VIEW DOCUMENT** command (SHFT F7, 6) takes the guessing game out of formatting (or designing the page layout of) your publication. **VIEW DOCUMENT** lets you preview on your computer screen how your advertisement, brochure or newsletter will look when it's printed.

You can evaluate your publication at three different levels of magnification, giving you the option of seeing the overall appearance of the page or focusing on smaller, selected areas in greater detail.

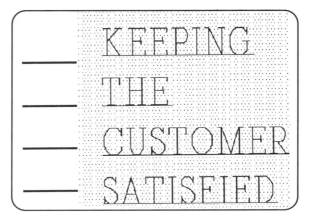

You can even view facing left- and right-hand pages—known as "spreads."

 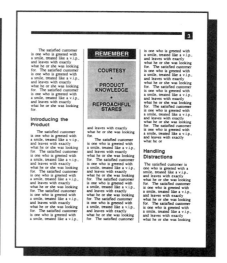

Because readers rarely encounter just one page at a time, the ability to look at spreads is an extremely important feature. WordPerfect's facing-pages feature helps ensure that left- and right-hand pages don't "fight" each other when viewed side by side.

Using Rules and Boxes

WordPerfect allows you to add rules—or lines—and boxes of any length and width anywhere on the page.

Rules and boxes are the basic building blocks of graphic design, which let you organize the various sections—or departments—of your publication in an attractive, logical way. They add to the visual appeal of your publication, help readers separate one feature from another and emphasize important ideas.

For example, WordPerfect makes it easy to add pull-quotes to your publication. Pull-quotes are short excerpts that summarize adjacent body copy and are usually set in large type in boxes.

You also can add sidebars—short features set in boxes that elaborate upon, or relate to, adjacent text. Depending upon the printer you use, you can even create boxes containing reversed headlines—white type on a black or screened background.

Adding Graphics to Your Documents

WordPerfect makes it easy to add—or import—charts, graphs and illustrations previously created with specialized drawing or image-scanning programs.

You can even place scanned photographs in your publications.

After graphics have been added, they can be made larger or smaller. In addition, you can distort them by increasing their height relative to the width, or vice versa.

Important parts of an imported graphics file can be emphasized by cropping—or moving the chart or illustration within its environment to eliminate unimportant elements.

You can rotate text or graphics files created with other software programs. For example, to create a special effect, you can place the masthead of your newsletter vertically on the page.

Locking Graphics with Text

With WordPerfect, you can link charts, graphs, illustrations, scanned photographs or selected text to either page position or adjoining paragraphs.

An illustration, for example, can be locked in the upper right-hand corner of a page and will remain there, regardless of how much adjoining text is added, deleted or edited.

Alternately, the illustration can be located to a specific paragraph. The illustration then "floats" with the paragraph. If preceding text is deleted, the illustration is pulled toward the beginning of the publication. If text is added, the illustration is pushed "along" with the paragraph. By locking a graphic to a specific paragraph, the graphic always is located next to the body copy it illustrates.

Locking Captions with Graphics

Just as you can lock graphics with text, WordPerfect permanently links captions with the charts, graphs, illustrations or scanned photographs they describe. This speeds up your work and makes it difficult for an illustration and its caption to become "lost." All captions automatically are placed in the same position relative to the graphic. You can choose to locate captions above or below the illustrations and align them with either the left- or right-hand borders, etc.

In addition, WordPerfect helps you create good-looking documents by automatically maintaining consistent spacing between captions and the charts, graphs, illustrations or photographs they describe. Readers are extremely sensitive to slight differences in spacing. Consistent spacing helps your publication look better and boosts readers' confidence in your message or product.

Furthermore, whenever you move a chart, graph, illustration or scanned photograph, its caption automatically moves to the new location.

Manipulating Text around Graphics

Text can be wrapped around or placed on top of charts, graphs, illustrations and scanned photographs. This further enhances your ability to create a distinct visual identity for your advertisement, brochure, newsletter, proposal or report.

Automatic text wrap means that the lines of type become shorter if they encounter a chart, graph or illustration. These lines are readjusted if you add or delete preceding text.

However, WordPerfect also gives you the option of superimposing text on top of an illustration or scanned photograph. This technique is useful when you're creating the cover of a brochure or adding explanations to illustrations in a training manual.

Borders and White Space

You can frame charts, graphs, illustrations, scanned photographs and text boxes with borders and white space.

Borders can be used to give your publication a distinct identity—appropriate for its overall purpose, as well as its design. Charts, graphs, illustrations and photographs can be surrounded by a wide choice of thick or thin lines, 100 percent black or screened to various shades of gray. You can even create dashed lines—useful for coupons.

Document Organization

WordPerfect goes far beyond most desktop publishing programs by offering highly sophisticated document organizing
abilities. It automatically generates a table of contents, index
and as many as nine different categories of lists.

You'll appreciate this power if you produce long documents,
such as books, software documentation or training manuals.

WordPerfect can perform in seconds, and with great accuracy,
organizational functions that normally would involve hours (if
not days) of tedious work.

The Reveal Codes Command

One of WordPerfect's most popular features has been its "clean
screen." Your words, and only your words, are visible on the
screen. Formatting codes are hidden in the background and
only become visible when a special **REVEAL CODES** command (ALT F3) is activated.

By using the **REVEAL CODES** command, you can see at a
glance which typeface and type size you're using, and whether
you're using boldface or italic type. If you have a color
monitor, typeface and type attributes (features) become even
more visible.

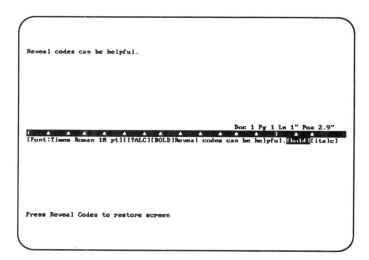

In earlier versions of WordPerfect, you couldn't edit (change) these codes while they were visible on your screen. WordPerfect now lets you edit while in **REVEAL CODES** mode, which simplifies formatting documents.

If you add the Hercules RamFont card (described in Appendix A), you can actually see accurate representations of the various type attributes as you apply them!

Formatting with Macros and Styles

WordPerfect's advanced macros and styles simplify formatting and reformatting documents.

For instance, WordPerfect's **STYLE** feature lets you assign in a single keystroke a specified typeface, type size, style and alignment for headlines and text.

When you access the **STYLE** command, all available styles are displayed, accompanied by a brief description of their intended application. You scroll down the list and select a style.

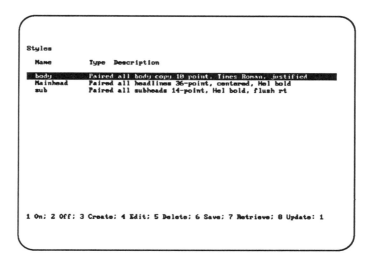

For example, you might want all headlines set in 36-point, centered, boldface Helvetica type, with reduced leading. You could store this setup as a **STYLE** called **MAINHEAD**.

ATTENTION!

For subheads, however, you might choose 14-point, Helvetica bold, italics, flush-right, with slightly reduced line spacing. Those decisions could be stored as a **STYLE** called **SUB**.

CREATING GREAT HEADLINES HAS NEVER BEEN EASIER

Body copy, however, might be set in 10-point, Times Roman type, with lines of equal length (justified). That could be saved as a **STYLE** identified simply as **BODY**.

WordPerfect styles can be applied at any point—while you write or edit, or later, after content has been finalized during the formatting stage.

WordPerfect's macros go even further, letting you repeat page layouts, including column alignments and graphic accents, such as rules, boxes and screens. Newsletter publishers, in particular, frequently use WordPerfect's macro capability.

WordPerfect's **MACRO** feature lets you quickly switch between a two- or three-column format, or turn off the column feature entirely to create headlines that span two or more columns. Macros also allow you to force white space between the top and bottom borders of a page, and add borders or publication information (e.g., page numbers and dates).

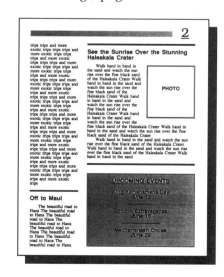

Macros simplify the process of creating screened boxes for sidebars or features, such as a table of contents or a calendar of upcoming events.

```
┌─────────────────────────────────┐
│        UPCOMING EVENTS          │
│                                 │
│      King Kamehameha Day        │
│           June 12               │
│        ───────────              │
│                                 │
│      London Extravaganza        │
│           June 16               │
│        ───────────              │
│                                 │
│      Mediterranean Cruise       │
│           June 29               │
└─────────────────────────────────┘
```

Enhanced Laser Printer Support

WordPerfect was one of the first word processing programs to take full advantage of the flexibility offered by laser printers. Laser printers form the basis of desktop publishing, allowing you to attain a quality of document previously associated only with expensive professional typesetting.

In the past, you only could create truly professional-looking documents by using a daisywheel printer. Daisywheel printers use a technology similar to that of an IBM Selectric typewriter. Each typeface comes on its own daisywheel. When you want to change typeface or type size, you physically have to remove the daisywheel and insert another, just as you would a type element in a Selectric.

Laser printers operate on an entirely different principle. Instead of using a mechanical (and often noisy) process of hitting an outline of each letter or number and having it create an image through a ribbon onto the paper, laser printers quietly create letters, numbers, charts, graphs and illustrations using a technology similar to that of office copiers. Letters, numbers and graphic images are created out of a grid three hundred dots high per inch and three hundred dots across.

Each laser printer has various type and graphics capabilities. Accessing them, however, often has been a time-consuming and tedious experience.

13

With WordPerfect 5.0 (and later versions), all available type-face, type size and type style alternatives are shown (in English) on your computer screen as you prepare your project.

No longer must you deal with arcane codes or strange ab-breviations. You can choose the particular characteristics by scrolling down the screen until the selection you want is highlighted. WordPerfect thus makes it easy to incorporate a variety of typefaces, type sizes and type styles into your document.

Typographic Refinements

WordPerfect offers precise control of letter and word spacing, necessary tools for creating good-looking advertisements, bro-chures and newsletters.

A special **ADVANCED PRINTER FUNCTIONS** command allows you to kern (adjust spacing between individual pairs of letters), which creates words out of isolated letters. Particularly important in designing headlines, kerning improves the appear-ance of large type and makes it easier to read.

With WordPerfect, you can expand or contract word and letter spacing throughout a document, which influences the color of your page. Adding extra letter and word spacing opens up a document, making it easier to read. Reducing letter and word spacing tightens a publication, increasing word density.

WordPerfect also lets you adjust line spacing, called leading, giving you more control over the vertical placement of type.

Leading is extremely important in creating high-impact headlines. If leading isn't modified, the lines of a headline often are spaced unnaturally. By letting you reduce line spacing, the headlines appear as strong, bold units, surrounded and emphasized by plenty of white space.

Type Alignment Alternatives

With WordPerfect, type can be placed on a page in four ways.

Flush-left/ragged-right text (in which the left-hand margin of type is aligned) often is used to create contemporary, open documents. Words are spaced equally on each line, creating a ragged right-hand margin. Flush-left/ragged-right type is used for both headlines and body copy.

Centered type often is used for headlines. Equal amounts of white space appear before and after each line.

Flush-right type (in which only the right-hand margin of type is aligned) often is used in multi-column documents to align subheads next to the body copy they introduce.

Flush-right type also is used in lists. In the example below, flush-right type makes it easy for readers to relate a job title to an individual's name.

Justified text occurs when all lines of text are the same length, with both the right and left margins aligned. In order to create lines of equal length, WordPerfect subtly adds or reduces word spacing within the line.

Shading and Reversing Type

Text can be reversed, screened or—depending upon your printer—printed in color.

SCRUMPTIOUS
SALADS

With an appropriate printer, WordPerfect lets you reverse headlines or departmental dividers, setting words in white against a black background.

WordPerfect's text-shading feature lets you achieve two-color effects at a one-color printing price. Brochure headlines, newsletter mastheads or departmental dividers within a book or training manual can be printed in various shades of gray, instead of 100 percent black.

In addition, WordPerfect is ready for the next generation of printers, now beginning to appear. When these become competitively priced, you'll be able to precisely mix the ink colors used for text, rules and boxes.

CREATING A NONSENSE FILE

Before you begin to explore WordPerfect 5.0's desktop publishing power, you may want to create a simple, unformatted file to call up when you want to experiment with various page layout and text manipulation capabilities.

To create this multi-page "nonsense" file,

Type: The quick brown fox jumped over the lazy dog. The quick brown fox jumped over the lazy dog. The quick brown fox jumped over the lazy dog. The quick brown fox jumped over the lazy dog. The quick brown fox jumped over the lazy dog. The quick brown fox jumped over the lazy dog. The quick brown fox jumped over the lazy dog.

Type: (RETURN)

Type: (HOME) (HOME) cursor control key

That brings you to the top of the section.

Type: ALT F4 **(HIGHLIGHT)**

Type: (HOME) (HOME) cursor control key

That brings you down to the bottom of the section.

Type: CTRL F4 **(MOVE)**

Select: Option 1 **(BLOCK)**

Select: Option 2 **(COPY)**

Type: (RETURN)

That adds another copy of the text to your cursor location.

Repeat this process several times. Notice how you block and save twice as much text each time. Your file quickly grows. Continue until you've created two or three pages of text. Then, save the file.

Type: F7 **(SAVE)**

Response: Save document?   (Y/N) Yes

Type: Y

Response: Document to be saved:

Type: AANONSEN

Type: (RETURN)

The "aa" prefix for the filename places the file at the top of your WordPerfect 5.0 subdirectory when you use the **LIST FILES** command (F5). That way you won't have to scroll through numerous files each time you want to load your "nonsense" file.

You now have a large, easy-to-find text file that you can use over and over again as you create different page layouts and explore WordPerfect's various typeface, type size and type style alternatives.

Eliminating Spelling Errors

Its built-in spell-checker gives WordPerfect a strong advantage as a desktop publishing program. Most dedicated page layout programs assume you're working with error-free text. They don't allow you to check the spelling of headlines, captions or text revisions that might have escaped a proofreader's scrutiny. As a result, typographic errors can slip in at the last minute.

WordPerfect's spell-checker eliminates that risk, giving you the capability of checking the spelling in your document at any point before you print it out.

Phonetic Commands

Contributing to WordPerfect 5.0's accessibility is its phonetic command capability, which allows you to select a WordPerfect command or option by typing either a number or a letter. For example, when choosing between a **HORIZONTAL LINE** (Option 1) and a **VERTICAL LINE** (Option 2) when you're in the **GRAPHICS** command, you either can enter the number of the option or the highlighted letter that summarizes the option (i.e., **H** for **HORIZONTAL** or **V** for **VERTICAL**).

These mnemonics—letters that represent words—are found throughout WordPerfect's menus and greatly simplify document editing and page layout.

Moving On

In this chapter, you've been introduced to just a few of Word-Perfect's new features that make it possible to create good-looking, easy-to-read documents. When you add those advantages to WordPerfect's already highly advanced and fast word-processing capabilities, you have a powerful work tool that will improve both the quality and speed with which you generate your print communications.

In the chapters that follow, you'll learn how to put Word-Perfect's desktop publishing features to work creating professional-looking advertisements, books, brochures, newsletters and training materials.

2

Basic Desktop Publishing Features

To begin your investigation of WordPerfect's desktop publishing capabilities, it's important to learn how easy it is to enhance the appearance of your documents by adding rules and boxes. Two of the most fundamental building blocks of graphic design, rules and boxes are likely to be often-repeated elements in your page layout, regardless of whether you're working on an advertisement, brochure, newsletter, book or training manual.

You'll also learn how WordPerfect's macro capabilities can expedite the placement of those graphics in your documents.

You can preview how those design elements look on the printed page by using WordPerfect's **VIEW DOCUMENT** feature. Let's start by exploring **VIEW DOCUMENT**. You'll then be able to see the fruits of your efforts as you create rules and boxes later in this chapter.

Previewing Finished Pages before Printing

One of WordPerfect's virtues has always been its "clean" screen, which lets you concentrate on writing and editing. However, as you begin working with page layouts, you may want to preview how your finished page—complete with rules, boxes and imported graphics—will look when it's printed.

To do that, open an existing file that contains two or more pages. (When experimenting with 5.0, you may want to use the "nonsense" file, created in Chapter One.) Then,

Type: SHFT F7 (**PRINT**)

Select: Option 6 (**VIEW DOCUMENT**)

Response: You'll see a reduced-size version of the finished page. Image detail is determined by the type of monitor you use. High-resolution monitors with VGA cards provide the most accurate displays.

WordPerfect lets you view your document at three different levels of magnification, as outlined below.

Select: Option 1 (**100%**)

This offers a view that's nearly the actual size of a portion of the page. Because the entire page is too large to be reproduced on your computer screen, you can move around the page by using the left/right and up/down cursor control keys. In addition, you can advance vertically through the document one screen at a time using the - or + cursor control keys.

Select: Option 2 (**200%**)

This provides a more detailed, close-up view of a smaller portion of the page. Again, you can move around, focusing on different parts of the page by using the left/right, up/down and - and + cursor control keys.

Select: Option 3 (**FULL PAGE**)

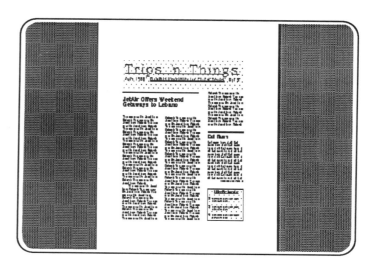

This provides a reduced, overall view of the full page, letting you review not only the placement of text and graphics, but the positioning of headers, footers and page numbers.

One of the most important rules in graphic design is to work in terms of two-page *spreads*. By doing so, you can avoid accidentally creating facing pages that "fight" each other. It's easy to design pages that look good by themselves, but look horrible when viewed side by side. WordPerfect's **FACING PAGES** feature helps you avoid that problem.

To move from Page 1 of your document to Pages 2 and 3 that face one another,

Type: (PAGE DOWN)

Select: Option 4 (**FACING PAGES**)

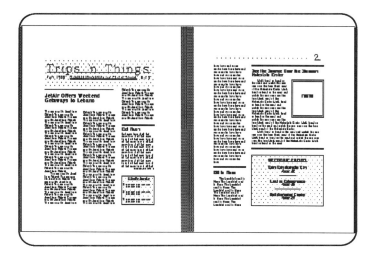

You now can view left-hand and right-hand pages side by side.

Moving around a Page

When viewing your document at 100 percent or 200 percent magnification, you'll be able to see only a portion of the page, unless you're using a big-screen monitor. As previously explained, the up/down, left/right cursor control keys, and the gray + and - keys let you view a different portion of the page.

Shortcuts

You also can use WordPerfect's **(HOME)** key in conjunction with the cursor control keys to quickly change your view of different parts of a page. These keyboard sequences are useful when working at large screen magnifications (100% and 200%). For example, **(HOME) (HOME)** Left Cursor Control Key advances your screen view to the left-hand side of a page. In a similar fashion, **(HOME) (HOME)** Right Cursor Control Key advances your screen view to the right-hand side.

To quickly move toward the top of the page you're previewing, use **(HOME) (HOME)** - . Likewise, **(HOME) (HOME) +** advances you toward the bottom of the page.

Viewing Different Pages

WordPerfect's **VIEW DOCUMENT** command offers two ways to scroll through multi-page documents, allowing you to see the progressive unfolding of your book, brochure, newsletter or training manual.

Type: (PAGE UP)

Response: This moves you to the previous page.

Type: (PAGE DOWN)

Response: This moves you to the next page.

You also can use WordPerfect's **GO TO** (CTRL HOME) command, followed by entering the page number you want to view.

Type: CTRL HOME   (**GO TO**)

Response: Go To

Type: The page number you want to preview.

Type: (RETURN)

Note that WordPerfect's status line in the lower right corner of the screen always indicates the page number, or numbers, you're viewing.

You also can use WordPerfect's **HOME** command to move quickly to the beginning or end of a document. To move to the end of a document,

Type: (HOME) (HOME)

Type: Down cursor control key

Response: You're moved to the last page of your document.

Alternately, to move to the beginning of a document,

Type: (HOME) (HOME)

Type: Up cursor control key

Response: You're moved to the first page of your document.

TIP: Remember that you cannot edit your document while in **VIEW DOCUMENT**; nor can you have both the **REVEAL CODES** and **VIEW DOCUMENT** functions operating simultaneously.

Exiting View Document

After previewing your work, touch the space bar to return to the **PRINT** menu. At that point, you'll probably choose one of the following three options:

- Option 1 (**FULL DOCUMENT**), if you want to print the entire document.

- Option 2 (**PAGE**), if you want to print just the page where your cursor is located.

- The space bar or (**RETURN**) to return to your document for continued text entry, editing or formatting.

Rules as Design Elements

Rules are lines of varying lengths, thicknesses and shading that serve many functions. They're used both to highlight important information as well as separate information. For example, the horizontal line under the headline strengthens and adds authority to the headline.

But, in the "Upcoming Events/Calendar" section of the following newsletter example, horizontal rules separate short topics from each other.

In newsletters and long documents, vertical rules often are used to separate columns.

Horizontal and vertical rules of various lengths also can be used to frame a page or an advertisement with attractive top, bottom and side borders.

WordPerfect makes it easy to add rules of varying lengths, thicknesses and shading to your documents. You can control where your rules are placed by using interactive menus that appear when you select the **GRAPHICS** command (ALT F9). By responding to the alternatives presented—for example, choosing Option 5 (**LINE**), followed by Option 1 (**HORI-ZONTAL LINE**) or Option 2 (**VERTICAL LINE**)—you easily can place a rule exactly where you want it.

Vertical Rules

WordPerfect makes it easy to add vertical lines to your documents. You can specify the placement, length, width and shading of these lines by simply choosing between the options presented to you after you select **GRAPHICS LINE** (ALT F9, 5), followed by **VERTICAL LINE** (Option 2).

Vertical lines easily can be drawn at any point on the page. Four options allow you to place the lines in the following locations:

1) **LEFT MARGIN**
2) **RIGHT MARGIN**
3) **BETWEEN COLUMNS**
4) **SET POSITION**

Option 4 (**SET POSITION**) lets you place lines by defining their position in inches from the left edge of the page, addressed below in Exercise One.

Exercise One: Adding Rules to Your Documents

Let's assume you want to add a rule in the left-hand margin of a document. To do that,

Type: ALT F9 (**GRAPHICS**)

Select: Option 5 (**LINE**)

Select: Option 2 (**VERTICAL LINE**)

Response: WordPerfect then displays the **VERTICAL LINE** menu.

Select: Option 1 (**HORIZONTAL POSITION**)

Response: **HORIZONTAL POSITION** options include:
Option 1 (**LEFT**)
Option 2 (**RIGHT**)
Option 3 (**BETWEEN COLUMNS**)
Option 4 (**SET POSITION**)

Select: Option 1 (**LEFT**)

Use WordPerfect's **VIEW DOCUMENT** command (SHFT F7, 6) to preview your work. You'll see that the vertical rule has been placed along the left-hand margin of the page.

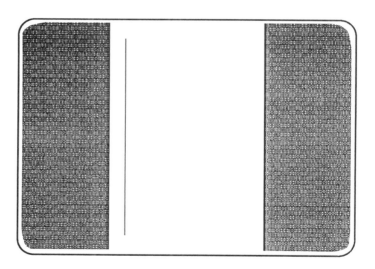

WordPerfect gives you total control over line placement. For example, you can describe the exact vertical position and line length.

Type: ALT F9 (**GRAPHICS**)

Select: Option 5 (**LINE**)

Select: Option 2 (**VERTICAL LINE**)

Select: Option 2 (**VERTICAL POSITION**)

Response: Option 1 (**FULL PAGE**) The line will extend from top to bottom of the page.

Option 2 (**TOP**) The line will extend down from the top of the page.

Option 3 (**CENTER**) The line will extend an equal length toward the top and bottom of the page from the center of the page.

Option 4 (**BOTTOM**) The line will extend up from the bottom of the page.

Option 5 (**SET POSITION**) You can define a specific starting point from the top of the page.

If you select an option other than the default, **FULL PAGE** (Option 1), you have to define the line length. For example, to center the four-inch-high line vertically along the left border of a page,

Select: Option 3 (**CENTER**)

Response: 9" This default extends a line the full height of the page.

Select: Option 3 (**LENGTH OF LINE**)

Type: 4

Type: (RETURN)

This replaces the nine-inch default with a four-inch line.

To make the line thicker,

Select: Option 4 (**WIDTH OF LINE**)

Response: 0.01"

Type: .25

This replaces the thin hairline with a quarter-inch-wide line.

Type: (RETURN)

Response: The result is a centered, quarter-inch-wide, four-inch vertical line along the left-hand margin of the page. You can see the line by using WordPerfect's **PRINT** (SHFT F7, 2) or **VIEW DOCUMENT** (SHFT F7, 6) commands.

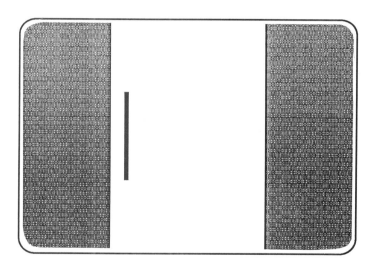

As the above example illustrates, trial and error may play an important role as you learn desktop publishing. Rather than resisting such efforts, welcome them. Only through experimentation will you become comfortable enough with WordPerfect to allow your talents to blossom. However, WordPerfect's **REVEAL CODES** (ALT F3) command can save a lot of time.

Using Reveal Codes

When you print your first desktop publishing exercise, the importance of WordPerfect's **REVEAL CODES** command becomes apparent. After previewing and printing your work, you might decide you want thicker or thinner, or longer or shorter, lines. WordPerfect's **REVEAL CODES** command (ALT F3) makes that simple to adjust.

Type: ALT F3 (**REVEAL CODES**)

Response: The screen now is divided horizontally. (The top portion contains only your text. The bottom, however, contains a definition that specifies the length and placement of the rule you've just created.)

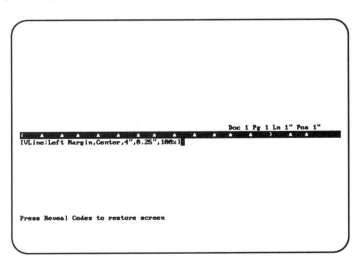

Note that when you use your cursor control keys, the cursor moves in both the "clean text" and **REVEAL CODES** areas of the screen.

To change the rule's appearance on the page, move the cursor until it highlights the definition specifying the length and placement of the rule you created in the **REVEAL CODES** screen. Delete the line definition with either the (**DELETE**) or backspace key. Then repeat the line creation process, changing line length or width specifications as desired.

Delete versus Backspace

While in **REVEAL CODES** note the difference between "delete" and "backspace." Use the (**DELETE**) key while the cursor is on the line definition. Use the backspace key when the cursor highlights the space immediately following the definition.

Leaving Reveal Codes

To return to the normal editing screen,

Type: ALT F3 (**REVEAL CODES**)

Response: You'll be returned to the original editing screen.

Note that being able to type **REVEAL CODES** (ALT F3) to return to your editing screen is a new feature of WordPerfect 5.0. Touching the space bar, or typing **EXIT** (F7) won't return you to the editing screen in Version 5.0.

Shaded Rules Add Document Color

As a design alternative, you might want to create rules in different shades of gray. Let's replace the vertical line drawn above with a line of the same length and thickness, but shaded to 60 percent of full black. The first step is to use WordPerfect's **REVEAL CODES** command to locate the original line definition and delete it. Then, draw a new line in its place.

Type: ALT F3 (**REVEAL CODES**)

Type: Use the up-down/left-right cursor control keys to locate the line definition above the headline in the **REVEAL CODES** screen.

Notice how the entire line definition is highlighted when the cursor touches it from either the left or right.

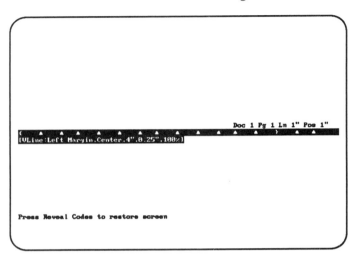

Type: (DELETE)

Response: This erases the entire line definition.

Now repeat the steps you went through above, but add one more step to the process. After you've created the line as described above, but before leaving the **VERTICAL LINE** menu,

Select: Option 5 (**GRAY SHADING (% OF BLACK)**)

Response: 100 %

Type: 60

Type: (RETURN)

Type: Space bar (This ends the line creation sequence.)

To return to a full editing screen,

Type: ALT F3 (**REVEAL CODES**)

To preview your shaded line, type **VIEW DOCUMENT** (SHFT F7, 6).

The difference should be quite noticeable. Gray rules add "color" in very apparent ways—yielding a two-color effect at a one-color cost. Compare the two illustrations below:

Macros and Line Creation

The more you use WordPerfect's many sophisticated options (line length, width, placement and shading options), the more you'll appreciate WordPerfect's macro capabilities. You can save a lot of time by turning on WordPerfect's **MACRO** command (ALT F10) and naming and defining a macro for each type of line before you create and place lines.

Simplifying Things with Macros

WordPerfect's macros further simplify the placement of rules. Consisting of command files, macros let you execute a complicated sequence of keystrokes by simply activating a one-word file.

Let's assume, for example, that the page layout you've designed for your employee training manual contains a quarter-inch-wide rule extending across the top of each page. Without WordPerfect's macro capability, you'd have to create this line from scratch on each page, or **BLOCK** (ALT F4) and **COPY** (CTRL F4, 1, 2), repeating the same keyboard commands each time. By simply creating a **TOPBORD** macro, as described below, you can add the border to the top of each page, eliminating the monotony of recreating it for each page of a document.

Exercise Two: Creating a Border Macro

Let's begin by creating a macro that adds a quarter-inch horizontal border along the top of each page.

Start by defining the **TOPBORD** macro. To activate the **DEFINE MACRO** command,

Type: CTRL F10 **(DEFINE MACRO)**

Response: Define macro

Type: TOPBORD

Type: (RETURN)

Response: Description

WordPerfect asks you for a macro description, a new 5.0 feature that helps you identify what each macro does, in case you forget. (Note: your description is limited to 39 characters.)

Type: Adds a 1/4-inch top border to each page

Type: (RETURN)

The flashing **MACRO DEF** prompt reminds you that all the keystrokes that follow will be memorized as part of the **TOPBORD** macro.

Now, place the cursor at the top of the page—or as far down from the top as you want the border to appear.

Type: ALT F9 (**GRAPHICS**)

Select: Option 5 (**LINE**)

Select: Option 1 (**HORIZONTAL LINE**)

Response: The WordPerfect **HORIZONTAL LINE** menu appears.

```
Graphics: Horizontal Line

    1 - Horizontal Position          Left & Right
    2 - Length of Line
    3 - Width of Line                0.01"
    4 - Gray Shading (% of black)    100%




Selection: 0
```

That menu allows you to define the line length, its alignment (left, right or centered), thickness and shading.

If you accept the default **LEFT AND RIGHT**, the line will extend from column to column over the entire page. (If you select Option 1 [**HORIZONTAL POSITION**], you'll be able to center the line, align it against either the left- or right-hand borders of the page or position it exactly where you want it from the left-hand margin of the page.)

Select: Option 3 (**WIDTH OF LINE**)

Then change the **0.01** default to **0.25**:

Type: 0.25

Press the space bar twice to close the file.

Type: CTRL F10 (to end the creation of your **TOPBORD** macro.)

Response: The **MACRO DEF** prompt disappears and you return to your document.

Previewing Your Work

Depending upon your monitor, the top border may or may not be visible on the screen. To make sure your rule has been placed in the correct position, use WordPerfect's **VIEW DOCUMENT** feature.

Type: SHFT F7 (**PRINT**)

Select: Option 6 (**VIEW DOCUMENT**)

Select: Option 3

The page now appears in reduced size on your screen with the quarter-inch border visible across the top of the page.

Adding the Border to the Following Pages

To add the border to the following pages, return to your document by pressing the space bar twice, then advance to the next page with the down cursor control key. At the top of each new page (indicated by the changing page number at the bottom right of your screen),

Type: ALT F10 (**MACRO**)

Response: Macro:

Type: TOPBORD

Type: (RETURN)

Response: The top border automatically is placed in the proper position.

NOTE: The top and bottom borders must be added *before* you create multiple columns (discussed in Chapter Three). Otherwise, borders only will extend the width of each column. (This can work to your advantage, however, when horizontal rules are used to separate items within a column.)

Introducing Another Way to Draw Lines

WordPerfect also offers a **LINE DRAW** command, accessed through the **SCREEN** command (CTRL F3). Lines drawn using the **LINE DRAW** command differ from lines created using WordPerfect's **GRAPHICS** command (ALT F9). Lines created using WordPerfect's **LINE DRAW** are drawn on the screen using the up/down, left/right cursor control keys. Although fewer thickness and shading options are available, you can draw lines with special characters (such as asterisks).

Lines created with **LINE DRAW** usually are visible immediately on the screen, whereas rules created with WordPerfect's **GRAPHICS** command often are made visible only by using WordPerfect's **VIEW DOCUMENT** feature. In addition, lines created with the **LINE DRAW** command can be edited with the (**DELETE**) and cursor control keys.

Printer limitations also are involved. Both lines and rules can be used in documents printed on Hewlett-Packard LaserJet Series II printers. However, lines created with WordPerfect's **LINE DRAW** command won't print on PostScript printers, such as the Apple LaserWriter Plus or the LaserWriter NT.

Other printer-to-printer and monitor-to-monitor variations involve creating a line out of special characters. However, you'll have to experiment with your particular monitor and printer to see just how much you can accomplish with the **LINE DRAW** feature.

Drawing Lines with Line Draw

To draw lines with your cursor control keys, place your cursor at the starting point of the line you want to draw. Then,

Type: CTRL F3 (**SCREEN**)

Select: Option 2 (**LINE DRAW**)

Select: Option 1 (**SINGLE LINE**)

Type: Use the left/right and up/down cursor control keys to draw either vertical or horizontal lines.

Note that corners automatically are created when you switch from horizontal to vertical cursor control keys. Small arrows appear at the beginning and end of each line you're drawing. (These arrows disappear when you **PRINT**.)

TIP: WordPerfect's **LINE DRAW** (CTRL F3, 2) command must be used very carefully, because it types over or deletes any text it encounters.

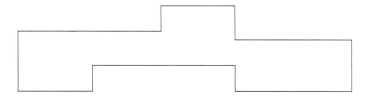

When you're finished,

Type: F7 (**EXIT**)

A similar procedure is used to draw double lines:

Type: CTRL F3 (**SCREEN**)

Select: Option 2 (**LINE DRAW**)

Select: Option 2 (**DOUBLE LINE**)

Type: Again, use the left/right and up/down cursor control keys to draw either vertical or horizontal lines.

Choose Option 3 (*) instead of Option 1 (**SINGLE LINE**) or (**DOUBLE LINE**), if you want to highlight important information with rows of asterisks. (The asterisk is a default that can be replaced by any other character, as described below.)

Changing Line Thickness or Shading

WordPerfect's 5.0's **LINE DRAW** command offers a limited number of variations on line thickness and shading.

Type: CTRL F3 (**SCREEN**)

Select: Option 2 (**LINE DRAW**)

Select: Option 4 (**CHANGE**)

Response: You're presented with nine options:

Option 1 Approximately 20 percent shaded, quarter-inch, horizontal, solid, one-eighth-inch vertical line.
Option 2 Approximately 50 percent shaded, one-quarter-inch, horizontal, solid, one-eighth-inch vertical line.
Option 3 Approximately 80 percent shaded, one-quarter-inch, horizontal, solid, one-eighth-inch vertical line.
Option 4 Full black, one-quarter-inch, solid, horizontal line with thin divisions every inch.
Option 5 Approximately one-eighth-inch, solid, horizontal line

with broken three-sixteenths-inch vertical line.

Option 6 Approximately one-quarter-inch, broken, horizontal line with solid, one-sixteenth-inch, vertical line.

Option 7 Approximately one-quarter-inch, shaded, broken, horizontal line with solid, one-sixteenth-inch, vertical line.

Option 8 Solid, approximately one-eighth-inch, horizontal line with three-sixteenths-inch, broken, vertical line.

Option 9 Allows you to use any letter or number or punctuation mark. WordPerfect responds with a **SOLID CHARACTER:** prompt to type the character you want to use.

Below are samples of Options 5 and 9.

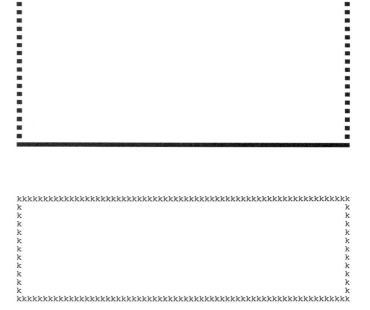

Erasing Lines and Moving the Cursor

When using the **LINE DRAW** feature, you can erase portions of the line you're working on by using the up/down, left/right cursor control keys from the current cursor position. While drawing lines,

Type: Option 5 (**ERASE**)

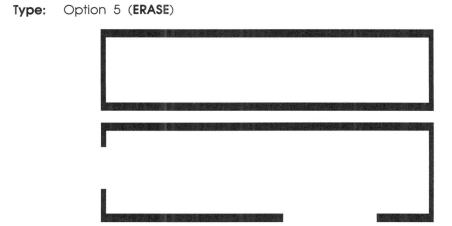

After you've exited the **LINE DRAW** command, you also can erase previously created lines. Simply place the cursor where you want to begin erasing and

Type: CTRL F3 (**SCREEN**)

Select: Option 2 (**LINE DRAW**)

Select: Option 5 (**ERASE**)

When using the **LINE DRAW** command, there may be times when you'd like to move the cursor with the cursor control keys without drawing a line. Option 6 (**MOVE**) makes that possible. At any point, while drawing lines,

Type: CTRL F3 (**SCREEN**)

47

Select:	Option 2 (**LINE DRAW**)
Select:	Option 6 (**MOVE**)
Response:	That lets you reposition the arrow control keys without drawing lines.

To resume drawing lines,

Select:	Option 1, 2, 3 or 4 (**Single**, **Double**, * or **Change**)

When you're finished,

Type:	F7 (**EXIT**)

Line Limitations

Remember that lines created with WordPerfect's **LINE DRAW** command (CTRL F3, 2) can be easily displaced. Words or spaces inserted in front of a vertical line, for example, "push" the line to the right.

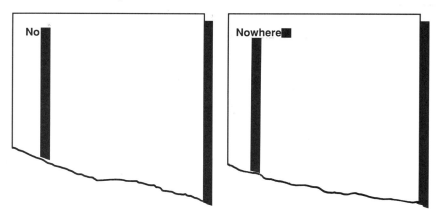

Likewise, backspaces or word deletions pull a vertical line to the left.

Boxes as Design and Layout Tools

Another fundamental building block of design is the box, which creates powerful, good-looking print communications. However, boxes can be somewhat confusing, because they refer both to one of the most commonly encountered graphic design tools, as well as one of WordPerfect's most important page layout tools.

Boxes as Design Elements

As graphic design tools, boxes are four-sided objects that can be used either to separate or draw attention to different categories of words.

For example, sidebars—short articles that accompany and support longer articles—are usually set in boxes to distinguish them from related text.

Pull-quotes—short sentences that summarize surrounding material—are another frequent application of boxes. Set in large type in a box within a page of text, pull-quotes provide visual contrast to long articles, as well as highlight important information. They're particularly useful in adding visual relief to a "gray" page when photos or illustrations aren't available.

Boxes can be used to draw attention to headlines, particularly reversed boxes that contain white type against a black background.

As a design tool, boxes can be used to isolate different categories of information. Many publications emphasize mailing and advertising information by setting it in a box.

Boxes can add impact to graphs, charts, illustrations and photographs.

Boxes also can be used as a design element to enclose page numbers.

You can use boxes to create coupons in advertisements.

Boxes as Layout Tools

In addition to their design function, boxes play an important role in WordPerfect's advanced page layout and document organization capabilities. WordPerfect uses boxes as "containers" for placing text, charts, graphs, drawings and scanned photographs. WordPerfect also uses boxes for placing mastheads and logos created with separate draw-type programs.

Boxes not only provide a framework for words and graphic images, they help WordPerfect organize documents, such as books with a lot of photographs and illustrations, proposals and reports containing charts and graphs, or training manuals with technical drawings. After you've finished editing your proposal, book or training manual, WordPerfect automatically can generate lists of graphics and indicate the page on which they appear, an important organizational tool to help readers locate information quickly.

WordPerfect gives you four ways to identify your boxes: **FIGURE**, **TABLE**, **TEXT** and **USER-DEFINED**. Note that words or graphic images can be entered into any type of box. The categories relate to the way WordPerfect numbers boxes when it generates lists of photographs, charts or tables at the conclusion of your project.

By providing both a structure for text and graphics, as well as organizing the contents of a document, boxes are crucial to WordPerfect's ability to smoothly integrate text and graphics into professional-looking, compelling documents.

Using Macros with Boxes

Just as macros expedite the placement of page borders, they also can be used to create and place boxes on a page. This can save a lot of time when numerous boxes of the same size have to be inserted into a document.

Exercise Three: Creating Graphics and Text Boxes

Let's start by creating a small box for a pull-quote, contained within a newsletter or magazine column. (For multi-column formatting, see Chapter Three.)

To start, place the cursor in the column where you want to insert the pull-quote. (If you're already familiar with WordPerfect, you'll know that to advance horizontally from column to column you use a combination of the **GO TO** command [CTRL-HOME] and the left and right cursor control keys.) You then vertically position the cursor with the up/down cursor control keys.

When the cursor is correctly positioned,

Type: ALT F9 (**GRAPHICS**)

Select: Option 3 (**TEXT BOX**)

Select: Option 1 (**CREATE**)

At this point, you have a decision to make. If you're creating a simple pull-quote, you need not assign it a filename. If you don't specify a filename, WordPerfect won't include this **TEXT BOX** in the list—or index—of **TEXT BOX**es that it compiles at the end of your project. However, to fill the box with text from another file—for example, if you're creating a sidebar and want its text to come from another file—you must assign the box a filename, if you want WordPerfect to keep track of its location. Next,

Select: Option 5 (**HORIZONTAL POSITION**)

You then are presented with various ways to place the **TEXT BOX** in or around the column. You'll probably choose either to center the **TEXT BOX** or have it extend from one column border to the other.

Select: Option 4 (**BOTH LEFT AND RIGHT**)

This creates a box that extends the width of the column.

Select: Option 6 (**SIZE**)

Select: Option 2 (**HEIGHT**)

Response: 0.7"

(This figure may vary slightly depending upon the dimensions of your page and the monitor you're using.)

Type: 1.5

Type: (RETURN)

That replaces the default with a box one-and-a-half inches high. Finally,

Select: Option 8 (**EDIT**)

Enter the text of your pull-quote.

Type: The quick brown fox jumped over the lazy dog.

Remember that you can change typeface, type size and type style attributes as you enter these words. Usually the type in a pull-quote is larger than the surrounding body copy. As you'll learn in Chapter Six, you can change typeface, type size and style by executing WordPerfect's **FONT** command (CTRL F8).

After you've entered and formatted your words,

Type: F7 (**EXIT**)

Press the space bar to return to your editing screen. Preview your work (SHFT F7, 6) or print out the page (SHFT F7, 2). It should be similar to the example below.

> **The quick brown fox jumped over the lazy dog.**

Notice that WordPerfect's **TEXT BOX** defaults include thick top and bottom bars, no side borders and a 10 percent screened background. To change these defaults, return to your editing screen and place the cursor in a position that precedes the box. Then,

Type: ALT F9 (**GRAPHICS**)

Select: Option 3 (**TEXT BOX**)

Select: Option 4 (**OPTIONS**)

Response: You're presented with the **TEXT BOX** option screen.

```
Options:    Text Box

    1 - Border Style
            Left                                  None
            Right                                 None
            Top                                   Thick
            Bottom                                Thick
    2 - Outside Border Space
            Left                                  0.16"
            Right                                 0.16"
            Top                                   0.16"
            Bottom                                0.16"
    3 - Inside Border Space
            Left                                  0.16"
            Right                                 0.16"
            Top                                   0.16"
            Bottom                                0.16"
    4 - First Level Numbering Method             Numbers
    5 - Second Level Numbering Method            Off
    6 - Caption Number Style                     [BOLD]1[bold]
    7 - Position of Caption                      Below box, Outside borders
    8 - Minimum Offset from Paragraph            0"
    9 - Gray Shading (% of black)                10%

Selection: 0
```

It includes a variety of **TEXT BOX** border treatments. Let's change the right- and left-hand borders to a single line.

Type: Option 1 (**BORDER STYLE**)

Response: You're offered a variety of options for the side border:

Option 1 (**NONE**)—default
Option 2 (**SINGLE**)

Option 3 (**DOUBLE**)
Option 4 (**DASHED**)
Option 5 (**DOTTED**)
Option 6 (**THICK**)
Option 7 (**EXTRA THICK**)

Select: Option 7 (**EXTRA THICK**)

Response: The highlight automatically jumps down to the right-hand border of the next line.

Select: Option 7 (**EXTRA THICK**)

Type: Enter (**RETURN**) twice to accept the default's thick borders for the top and bottom borders.

Adding a Screen to a Box

Before you leave the **TEXT BOX OPTIONS** definition screen, notice that the default shading for **TEXT BOX**es is 10 percent. You can add impact to your pull-quote by choosing a darker screen.

Select: Option 9 (**GRAY SHADING (% OF BLACK)**)

Response: The cursor now appears under the 10 percent default.

Type: 40

Type: (RETURN)

The resulting pull-quote should resemble the example below.

Remember, these changes do not have to be repeated: They

will remain in effect for each of the **TEXT BOX**es that follows.

Creating Sidebars

As previously mentioned, larger **TEXT BOX**es can be created to accommodate separate articles in a newsletter, cautionary tips in a training manual or a calendar of upcoming events in a newspaper. The principles are the same as those you just used to create a pull-quote. However, the dimensions of the **TEXT BOX** are larger.

Sidebars often are used as containers for integrating existing text files into a document. Let's assume you previously created a text file saved under the filename, **JOURNAL**. To place it in the publication you're currently working on,

Type: ALT F9 (**GRAPHICS**)

Select: Option 3 (**TEXT BOX**)

Select: Option 1 (**CREATE**)

Select: Option 1 (**FILENAME**)

Type: JOURNAL (or another filename for an existing text file.)

Type: (RETURN)

Type: Space bar (to return to editing your document.)

Preview your work on the screen (SHFT F7, 6) or print out the page (SHFT F7, 2).

Exercise Four: Resizing Text Boxes

In some cases, you might find that the **TEXT BOX** either isn't large enough to accommodate your text file or is too large. WordPerfect makes it easy to modify the dimensions of **TEXT BOX**es after they've been created. Start by executing the **GRAPHICS** command:

Type: ALT F9 (**GRAPHICS**)

Select: Option 3 (**TEXT BOX**)

Select: Option 2 (**EDIT**)

Response: Text box number? 1

Type: (RETURN)

Select: Option 6 (**SIZE**)

Response: You'll be offered the following options:

Option 1 (**WIDTH (AUTO HEIGHT)**)
Option 2 (**HEIGHT (AUTO WIDTH)**)
Option 3 (**BOTH WIDTH AND HEIGHT**)

Select: Option 2

Type: 8 (This replaces the default with the estimated eight-inch height of your sidebar.)

Type: (RETURN)

Preview your work on screen (SHFT F7, 6) or print the page (SHFT F7, 2) to check the accuracy of your space estimate. Repeat the above process, lengthening or shortening the height of the box, until it's just large enough to contain the text file you're importing.

Graphics Boxes

Graphics boxes are used when you want to place a previously created file into your document. This file can be an illustration, a scanned photograph, or a masthead or logo created with a draw-type program.

The principles of creating a graphics box are the same as those used to create **TEXT BOX**es, although more options are available for adjusting the placement of the graphic image in the box. Captions also are more important with **FIGURE** or **TABLE BOX**es.

Modifying imported text and graphics files is such an important issue that an entire chapter is devoted to the subject. (See Chapter Five.) For purposes of illustration, however, let's simply review the process.

Exercise Five: Creating a Graphics Box

Let's place the previously drawn clock illustration into a box. (**CLOCK** is stored in a file named **CLOCK.WPG,** included with WordPerfect 5.0.) Start by moving the cursor to the column and vertical location where you want to insert a graphic image.

Select: ALT F9 (**GRAPHICS**)

Select: Option 1 (**FIGURE**)

Response: Figure Menu

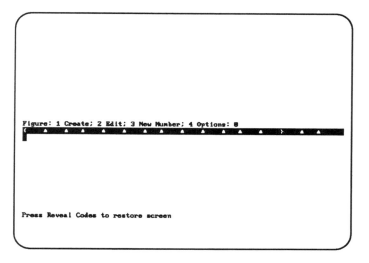

When the **FIGURE** menu appears,

Select: Option 1 (**CREATE**)

Select: Option 1 (**FILENAME**)

Type: Enter the filename—in this case, **CLOCK.WPG**

Type: (RETURN)

Select: Option 2 (**CAPTION**)

Next, enter the caption for the illustration:

Type: "An example of a frequently used means of telling time."
(Be sure to put one or more spaces before the caption to separate it from **Figure 1**. Otherwise, there will be no space between the figure number and the beginning of the caption. Longer captions will print automatically on the line beneath the figure number.)

In Chapter Five, you'll learn how to choose a particular typeface, type size, type style and alignment for your captions. In Chapter Eight, you'll learn how to save these attributes as a **STYLE** which will simplify the process of achieving consistency throughout your document.

Select: F7 (**EXIT**)

Now, to specify the illustration's position in the column,

Select: Option 5 (**HORIZONTAL POSITION**)

Select: Option 4 (**BOTH LEFT AND RIGHT**)

Response: This centers the box in the column.

Type: F7 (**EXIT**) (to exit your document.)

To view the placement of the graphics box, return to the document and

Type: SHFT 7, 6 (**VIEW DOCUMENT**)

If you'd like to print the document,

Type: SHFT F7, 2 (**PRINT PAGE**)

Locking Box Location

WordPerfect offers two ways to place boxes in your document. You can choose to lock boxes to specific page locations or to the surrounding text.

When locked to specific page locations, box positions remain unchanged, even if the text surrounding them changes during last-minute document editing. When a box is locked to surrounding text, however, the box follows the text to which it's set, regardless of its column or page position. Boxes also can be locked to specific sentences.

When there isn't space for a paragraph-locked box to be printed in a column or on a page, the paragraph and accompanying box automatically move to the next column or page.

To lock a box of any type—whether it be words, illustrations or a numeric table—to a specific location on a page,

Type: ALT F9 (**GRAPHICS**)

Select: Either Option 1 (**FIGURE**), Option 2 (**TABLE**), Option 3 (**TEXT BOX**) or Option 4 (**USER-DEFINED BOX**), depending upon the category of your box.

Select: Option 1 (**CREATE**)

Select: Option 3 (**TYPE**)

Response: You're presented with the following choices:

Select Option 1 (**PARAGRAPH**) if you want to lock the box and its caption to an adjacent paragraph.

Select Option 2 (**PAGE**) if you want the box and its caption to be locked into a specific position on that particular page.

Select Option 3 (**CHARACTER**) if you want to lock the box and its contents to a particular location in a sentence. This option often is used for page numbers or to create large initial caps.

The following examples show the difference between page-locked, paragraph-locked and character-locked boxes.

This shows a graphics box placed on the page.

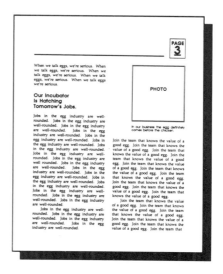

This is how the page appears after a paragraph has been deleted (Option 2).

This is how the page appears when the box is character-locked (Option 3).

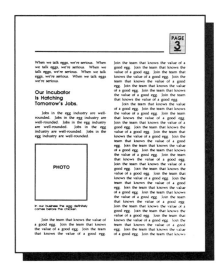

Deleting Boxes and Their Contents

Use WordPerfect's **REVEAL CODES** (ALT F3) to delete a box from a page after it has been created. Simply advance the cursor until the box number, filename and caption are highlighted, then delete.

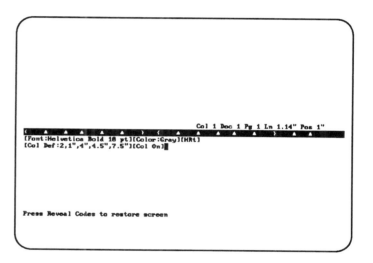

TIP: Exercise extreme care when removing boxes. After you've deleted a box using the (**DELETE**) key, it cannot be restored with WordPerfect's **CANCEL** command (F1).

Replacing the Contents of a Graphics Box

Instead of deleting the contents of **FIGURE BOX**, leaving the box intact but empty, you can replace its contents with another previously created graphics image. Here's the sequence of steps to follow:

Type: ALT F9 (**GRAPHICS**)

Select: Option 1 (**FIGURE**)

Select: Option 2 (**EDIT**)

Response: Figure Number? 2 (or the number of the last **TEXT BOX** created n that page. If your cursor is on a following page, however, the default number will be one higher than the number of the last **TEXT BOX** created.)

Type: 1 (Replace the default number with the number of the **FIGURE BOX** you want to edit.)

Type: (RETURN)

Response: Again, you'll be presented with the **FIGURE** definition menu which contains the name of the previously placed file, **CLOCK.WPG** (**GRAPHICS**).

Select: Option 1 (**FILENAME**)

Type: ARROW1.WPG (It replaces **CLOCK.WPG.**)

Type: (RETURN)

Response: Replace contents with ARROW1.WPG? (Y/N) No

Type: Y

Again, the space bar returns you to your editing screen.

Deleting Box Contents

To delete the contents of a box, but leave its placement intact,

Type: ALT F9 (**GRAPHICS**)

Then, select the type of box you want to edit. You're presented with the following choices: Option 1 (**FIGURE**), Option 2 (**TABLE**), Option 3 (**TEXT**) or Option 4 (**USER-DEFINED**). In this case, let's eliminate the clock figure from our first **FIGURE BOX**.

Select: Option 1 (**FIGURE**)

Select: Option 2 (**EDIT**)

Response: Figure Number? 2 (If the cursor is on the page containing a graphics box, WordPerfect defaults to the number of the last box created. If your cursor is on a following page, WordPerfect defaults to one number higher than the number of the last box created.)

To replace the default with the box number you want to modify,

Type: 1

Type: (RETURN)

Response: You're presented with the **FIGURE** definition menu which contains the name of the imported file, **CLOCK.WPG** (**GRAPHICS**).

Select: Option 1 (**FILENAME**)

Type: Use your (**DELETE**) key to erase the filename, **CLOCK.WPG**.

Type: (RETURN)

Response: Clear Contents? (Y/N) No

Type: Y (This verifies your intention to delete the contents of **FIGURE BOX 1**, but leave the box in its present position.)

Type: Space bar

The space bar returns you to your editing screen.

Again, remember that this is an irreversible step. You won't be able to restore the contents of the box with WordPerfect's **CANCEL** command (F1).

Editing Text Boxes

A similar procedure is used to edit, or replace, the contents of a **TEXT BOX**. Let's edit the **TEXT BOX** created above.

Type: ALT 9 (**GRAPHICS**)

Select: Option 3 (**TEXT BOX**)

Select: Option 2 (**EDIT**)

Response: Text Box number: 1

Again, the default is the number of the last **TEXT BOX** created on that page, or one number higher than the last box created if the cursor is on a following page.

Type: 1 (Enter the number of the **TEXT BOX** you want to edit.)

Type: (RETURN)

Response: You'll be presented with the **TEXT BOX** definition menu that lets you modify its size, placement and contents.

Type: 8 (**EDIT**)

Response: The original text of the pull-quote now appears on the screen.

Edit, delete or replace these words with other words. When you're finished,

Type: F7 (**EXIT**)

The space bar returns you to the editing screen.

In Chapter Five, you'll learn ways of manipulating imported graphics, such as moving the image within the box, reducing or enlarging image size, rotating the image, changing background and frames, as well as ways of adjusting the distance between the contents of a box and its boundaries. You'll learn about the Clipboard feature, found in the WordPerfect Library, which imports previously prepared graphic images.

Using Boxes to Control White Space

Because WordPerfect automatically wraps type around boxes (unless that feature is defeated), **USER-DEFINED BOX**es can be an extremely powerful design tool. They can be used to control white space at the top, bottom and sides of a page.

USER-DEFINED BOXes control white space because they have neither borders nor inside shading (unless you use the **USER-DEFINED BOX** option [ALT F9, 4, 4] to change the defaults). Constructed with WordPerfect's normal defaults, **USER-DEFIN-ED BOX**es force text to wrap around them—creating precisely placed blocks of white space—even though the boxes them-selves don't show up on the printed page.

For example, a two-inch sink—or band of white space—at the top of a page and a one-inch sink at the bottom can be created by using an invisible **USER-DEFINED BOX**.

As you read the following, remember that if you use WordPer-fect's **CREATE MACRO** feature (CTRL 10), keystrokes will be recorded in a macro file, allowing the boxes to be easily repeated on every page of your document.

Creating a Two-inch Sink

Advance your cursor to a new page—or start a new file.

Type: ALT F9 (**GRAPHICS**)

Select: Option 4 (**USER-DEFINED BOX**)

Select: Option 1 (**CREATE**)

Select: Option 3 (**TYPE**)

Select: Option 2 (**PAGE**)

This locks the box to the same position on each page, regard-less of text editing.

Select: Option 5 (**HORIZONTAL POSITION**)

Select:	Option 1 (**MARGINS**)
Select:	Option 4 (**BOTH LEFT AND RIGHT**)
Response:	The size will appear 6.5" wide x 6.5" high. (This is obviously too large!)
Select:	Option 6 (**SIZE**)
Select:	Option 3 (**BOTH WIDTH AND HEIGHT**)
Response:	Width = 6.5"
Type:	(RETURN) (This accepts the default, so the box will extend from margin to margin.)
Response:	Height = 6.5"
Type:	2 (This replaces the 6.5-inch-high box with a 2-inch-high box that forces the top of each column of type two inches down from the top of the page.)
Type:	(RETURN) (This returns you to the text editing screen. Your box has been placed.)

Note that you won't be able to see this box using the **VIEW DOCUMENT** command (SHFT F7, 6). That's because the default setting for **USER-DEFINED BOX**es has neither borders nor inside shading.

However, if you were to place type on the page at this point, it would look like this:

Adding White Space at the Bottom of Each Page

A similar process can be used to control where text appears on each page. To create a one-inch margin of white space at the bottom of each page:

Type: ALT F9 (**GRAPHICS**)

Select: Option 4 (**USER-DEFINED BOX**)

Select: Option 1 (**CREATE**)

Select: Option 3 (**TYPE**)

Select: Option 2 (**PAGE**)

To ensure that the box appears in the same position on each page:

Select: Option 4 (**VERTICAL POSITION**)

Select: Option 4 (**BOTTOM**)

Select: Option 5 (**HORIZONTAL POSITION**)

Select: Option 1 (**MARGINS**)

Select: Option 4 (**BOTH LEFT AND RIGHT**)

Response: The size again appears 6.5" wide by 6.5" high.

Select: Option 6 (**SIZE**)

Select: Option 3 (**BOTH WIDTH AND HEIGHT**)

Response: Width = 6.5"

Type: (RETURN) (This accepts the default, so the box will extend from margin to margin.)

Response: Height = 6.5"

Type: 1

Type: (RETURN)

Press the space bar to return to your editing screen.

This replaces the 6.5-inch-high box with a one-inch-high box extending from margin to margin of white space and returns you to the text editing screen.

To see how these boxes perform, add some text to the page. The easiest way to do that is to move your cursor to the top of the page, under the "USR1" line (if it's visible—which depends upon your monitor) and enter some text, or place a previously completed WordPerfect text file.

Type: F5 (**LIST FILES**)

Response: The current default directory appears.

An alphabetical list of previously stored WordPerfect files residing in the default directory will appear. If this is the directory where you've stored a file,

Type: (RETURN)

Otherwise, change to another subdirectory, containing previously completed work.

Scroll down until you highlight the previously completed text file you want to place. (You might want to choose the **AANONSEN** file you created in Chapter One.)

Select: Option 1 (**RETRIEVE**)

Response: Retrieve into current document? (Y/N) No

Type: Y

Response: Text will flow down the page, beginning two inches from the top of the page and ending one inch from the bottom.

Adding White Space to the Side of Each Page

A similar technique can be used to create a block of white space to the left of your body copy, which is useful for letterheads. It also can be used for brochures, books or training manuals because you can go back later and place subheads in the white space.

Let's create a **USER-DEFINED BOX** that adds two inches of white space to the left of each column of text.

Type:	ALT F9 (**GRAPHICS**)
Select:	Option 4 (**USER-DEFINED BOX**)
Select:	Option 1 (**CREATE**)
Select:	Option 3 (**TYPE**)
Select:	Option 2 (**PAGE**)

To ensure that the box appears in the same position on each page,

Select:	Option 4 (**VERTICAL POSITION**)
Select:	Option 1 (**FULL PAGE**)
Select:	Option 5 (**HORIZONTAL POSITION**)
Select:	Option 1 (**MARGINS**)
Select:	Option 1 (**LEFT**)
Select:	Option 6 (**SIZE**)
Response:	Width = 2.16"
Type:	2
Type:	(RETURN)

Response: Height = 9"

Type: (RETURN)

Response: 2" wide by 9" high

Type: (RETURN)

This returns you to the text editing screen.

Again, place a previously written text file (e.g., **AANONSEN**) on the page. Notice how two inches of white space now appear in the left-hand border of the page, as the text wraps around the invisible **USER-DEFINED BOX**.

TIP: It's important that these boxes be created while you're in a single-column mode. If you try to create them while using WordPerfect's multi-column feature (see Chapter Three), the boxes only will extend the width of the current column.

White-space boxes can be created at any time—before or after text has been entered. When created after text has been entered, the white-space boxes will push the text out of the way.

In a later chapter, you'll see how macros can expedite the page layout process by allowing you to automatically place white-space boxes on as many pages as necessary before text is placed.

Superimposing Boxes on Top of Each Other

Although you cannot create boxes within boxes, you can superimpose boxes, which means you can place text or graphics boxes in the white space of previously created boxes. You can add headline text within the white space defining the top of the page or place illustrations and captions within a band of white space to the left of your body copy.

Text or graphics boxes must be placed within other boxes by measurement, since you cannot create a box on top of a pre-existing one. To understand the process, let's import a graphic and place it in the left-hand white-space box created above.

Type: ALT F9 (**GRAPHICS**)

Select: Option 1 (**FIGURE**)

Select: Option 1 (**CREATE**)

Select: Option 1 (**FILENAME**)

Type: CLOCK.WPG

Type: (RETURN)

Select: Option 2 (**CAPTION**)

Type: The preferred method of telling time when hourglasses aren't available.

Type: F7 (**EXIT**)

Select: Option 3 (**TYPE**)

Select: Option 2 (**PAGE**)

Select: Option 4 (**VERTICAL POSITION**)

Select: Option 5 (**SET POSITION**)

Response: Offset from top of page: 1"

Type: 3.25

Type: (RETURN)

Select: Option 5 (**HORIZONTAL POSITION**)

Select: Option 1 (**MARGINS**)

Select: Option 1 (**LEFT**)

Select: Option 6 (**SIZE**)

Select: Option 1 (**WIDTH (AUTO HEIGHT)**)

Response: Width = 2.16"

Type: 1.75

Type: (RETURN)

Reducing the size of the **FIGURE BOX** adds white space between the illustration and adjacent body copy.

Type: (RETURN)

This returns you to the editing screen.

Type: SHFT F7 (**PRINT**)

Select: Option 6 (**VIEW PAGE**)

The result should appear as follows:

As you'll see in Chapter Five, rules and boxes also can be superimposed over existing white-space boxes, letting you create a variety of good-looking borders for your pages. You also can add **TEXT BOX**es within whitespace boxes, allowing you to place headlines and subheads adjacent to body copy.

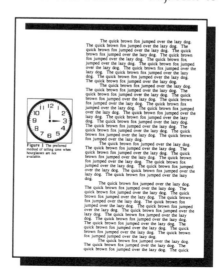

White-space boxes can be used to ensure accurate spacing between titles or headlines and the body copy they introduce, or between articles within newsletter columns. White-space boxes can also be used to create the first pages of chapters in a book.

In each case, WordPerfect's macro capability lets you store your white-space boxes as files, so that you easily can repeat these valuable graphics tools on each page.

Moving On

As you become increasingly involved with desktop publishing, you'll probably use WordPerfect's extensive line and box creation and editing capabilities frequently.

Next, let's take a closer look at WordPerfect's formatting capabilities—such as its ability to create multi-column documents—and the polished image and flexibility columns can add to your design.

3

Working with Multi-column Layouts

In this chapter, you'll be introduced to a major WordPerfect enhancement: the ability to create multi-column documents. Perhaps no design element is as important to producing professional-looking advertisements, booklets, brochures and newsletters as the ability to combine multi-column formats with rules of different lengths, widths and shades of gray. These features make it easy to construct documents that are attractive, readable and have a great deal of design flexibility.

Creating Multiple Columns

It's a rare newsletter or manual that extends type from one page margin to another in a single, unbroken line. Effective, good-looking print communications usually are characterized by multiple columns of type—typically formatted in two or more parallel columns.

WordPerfect makes it easy to create page layouts with columns. You can place as many as twenty-four columns on each page. Columns can be of the same or differing widths.

To create a multi-column document,

Type: ALT F7 (**MATH/COLUMN**)

Select: Option 4 (**COLUMN DEF**)

Response: WordPerfect's **TEXT COLUMN** definition screen appears.

```
Text Column Definition

  1 - Type                              Newspaper

  2 - Number of Columns                 2

  3 - Distance Between Columns

  4 - Margins

  Column    Left      Right     Column    Left      Right
    1:      1"        4"          13:
    2:      4.5"      7.5"        14:
    3:                            15:
    4:                            16:
    5:                            17:
    6:                            18:
    7:                            19:
    8:                            20:
    9:                            21:
   10:                            22:
   11:                            23:
   12:                            24:

Selection: 0
```

At this point, define the type of columns you want to create.

Select: Option 1 (**TYPE**)

Response: You're presented with the three types of columns. Make your selection and press (**RETURN**).

If you choose Option 1 (**NEWSPAPER**), text will flow from the bottom of one column to the top of the next column, filling each column in sequence until the page is filled. Type then continues to the top of the first column on the following page. Newspaper columns frequently are used for newsletters, books and magazines.

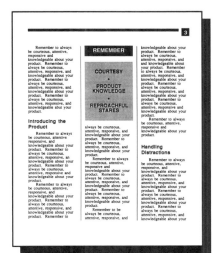

Choose Option 2 (**PARALLEL**) if you're creating documents in which information must be organized horizontally and the amount of copy in each column is likely to be different. If there's too much text to fit in a column on one page, the text will continue in the same column on the next page.

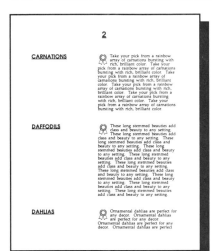

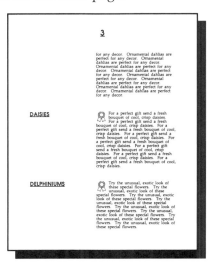

Choose Option 3 (**PARALLEL WITH BLOCK PROTECT**) if you don't want information within a column separated, or continued, from one page to another. If your text is too long to fit on a page, the entire entry—text in all adjacent columns—will move automatically to the next page. These columns often are used for price lists or inventory lists, in which text blocks or item descriptions must be kept together.

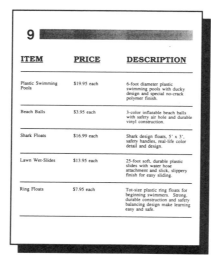

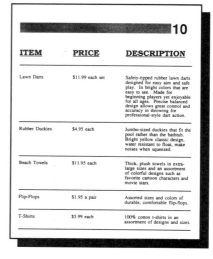

Column Placement and Spacing

After you've selected the type of columns you want, you must determine their placement and spacing.

Column width, placement and spacing greatly influence the appearance and readability of your publications. As discussed in Chapter Ten, "Planning and Producing Your Documents," column width should relate to the type size you're planning to use. In general, narrow columns work well with small type sizes, and wider columns work well with larger type sizes.

a) Small type placed in wide columns is difficult to read because the reader gets lost between the end of one line and the beginning of the next.

7-point text placed on a 24-pica column is very difficult to read. 7-point text placed on a 24-pica column is very difficult to read. 7-point text placed on a 24-pica column is very difficult to read. 7-point text placed on a 24-pica column is very difficult to read. 7-point text placed on a 24-pica column is very difficult to read. 7-point text placed on a 24-pica column is very difficult to read. 7-point text placed on a 24-pica column is very difficult to read. 7-point text placed on a 24-pica column is very difficult to read. 7-point text placed on a 24-pica column is very difficult to read. 7-point text placed on a

b) Large type in narrow columns leads to excessive hyphenation and gaps between words.

Your choice of justified or flush-left/ragged-right type also should influence column width.

16-point text placed on a 12 pica column is also very difficult to read.

Justified type occurs when the last letter of the last word in each line are aligned, making each line of type the same length.

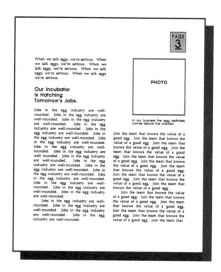

Flush-left/ragged-right type is characterized by lines of irregular length.

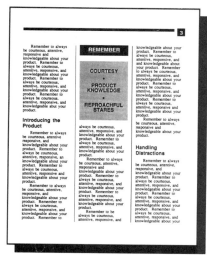

Because justified columns form more distinct visual elements, less space is needed between them than is necessary with flush-left/ragged-right columns.

Another design consideration to take into account concerns rules. If you plan to add vertical rules between the columns, extra space must be added.

Creating Multi-column Documents

To create a multi-column publication,

Select: Option 2 (**NUMBER OF COLUMNS**)

Response: 2

Type: 3

Type: (RETURN)

By entering a different number, you've replaced WordPerfect's default with the number of columns you want. Notice that when you replace the two-column default with a different number, column spacing automatically changes.

Next, define the distance between columns.

Select: Option 3 (**DISTANCE BETWEEN COLUMNS**)

Response: .5

Type: .75

Type: (RETURN)

This replaces the half-inch column spacing with a three-quarter-inch gutter—space between columns. Notice that the column widths automatically change to compensate for increased or decreased column spacing.

Setting Individual Column Widths

One of the most important column definition functions is Option 4 (**MARGINS**), which lets you create columns of different widths. It also lets you determine where each column will be placed in relation to page boundaries.

Notice how the cursor immediately jumps to the left dimension of the first column. To accept the default dimension, which WordPerfect computes on the assumption that all columns are of equal width,

Type: (RETURN)

Response: This accepts the default and advances the cursor to the right-hand margin of the first column.

To create a narrow left-hand column for subheads,

Type: 2 (This replaces the 2.66-inch, right-hand default with a narrower column.)

Type: (RETURN) (This advances the screen to let you adjust the left-hand margin of the second column.)

Type: 2.75

Type: (RETURN)

Response: This advances the screen to let you adjust the right-hand margin of the second column.

Type: 4.25

Type: (RETURN)

Response: This advances the screen to let you adjust the left-hand margin of the third column.

Type: 4.5

Type: (RETURN)

This replaces the default setting with the setting necessary for the second wide column. It also advances the screen to the position where you can adjust the right-hand margin of the right-hand column. To accept this default,

Type: (RETURN)

Working with Multiple Columns

Once you've defined the column format you want, turn on WordPerfect's multi-column feature. Otherwise, the text you enter will continue to extend in an unbroken line from the left-hand margin of the page to the right-hand margin. You may find yourself frequently switching back and forth between single- and multi-column formats as you add graphic accents or previously created charts, graphs, illustrations or scanned photographs.

For example, you must be in a single-column mode if you want to add horizontal bars as borders at the top and bottom of each page. You also must be in a single-column format if you want to add a large headline that will span all of the columns on a page.

After you've defined the size and placement of each column, accept your column definitions by hitting the space bar or (**RETURN**).

You're then brought back to the initial **MATH/COLUMNS** menu. To activate a multi-column format,

Select: Option 3 (**COLUMN ON/OFF**)

Option 3 (**COLUMN ON/OFF**) toggles, or switches, your page format back and forth between single-column and multi-column format.

If you're working in a multi-column setting and want to return to a single-column format,

Type: ALT F7 (**MATH/COLUMNS**)

Select: Option 3 (**COLUMN ON/OFF**)

Response: This returns you to a single-column format.

If, however, you're working in a single-column format and want to return to a multi-column format,

Type: ALT F7 (**MATH/COLUMNS**)

Select: Option 3 (**COLUMN ON/OFF**)

Response: You're returned to your previously defined multi-column format.

Moving from Column to Column

With WordPerfect, it's easy to advance from one column to the next column during text entry or editing. When entering text with **NEWSPAPER** columns, your cursor automatically advances to the top of the next column when you reach the bottom of a column.

HARD PAGE (CTRL RETURN) advances you from one column to another when you enter text with **PARALLEL** columns.

If you enter new text after WordPerfect's **COLUMN** feature has been activated, the text automatically will be placed in the correct column. If, however, you define and activate a column layout after text has been entered, you must execute WordPerfect's **SCREEN REWRITE** command (CTRL F3, 0). Otherwise, the text will remain unformatted, extending from side to side on your screen until you advance the cursor through the text. To execute this command,

Type: CTRL F3 (**SCREEN**)

Select: Option 0 (**REWRITE**)

Moving between Columns

When editing text, you can move back and forth between columns by using WordPerfect's **GO TO** command (CTRL HOME), followed by the right or left cursor control keys. For example, to move to the next column on the right,

Type: CTRL (HOME)

Type: Right cursor control key

To move to the column on the left,

Type: CTRL (HOME)

Type: Left cursor control key

When editing multi-column documents, the up/down cursor control and (**DELETE**) keys are only active within each column. Thus, if you're in column one, WordPerfect's popular **DELETE TO END OF PAGE** command (CTRL PG DN) will only erase text in that column.

When working in multi-column text, the status line at the lower right of your screen indicates the column in which you're working. For example, **Col 1** shows that the cursor is located in the first column on the page.

Next Column Command

When working with newspaper-type columns, WordPerfect's **HARD PAGE** command (CTRL RETURN) makes it easy to end one column and begin the next. Use **HARD PAGE** when you want subsequent text placed in the next column. This is particularly useful if you want to make the first column shorter than the others. For example, you can use this feature to isolate subheads in the first column of training manuals.

Creating Justified Columns

Before entering text in a column, you must switch between flush-left/ragged-right columns and justified text. To reactivate column justification if you've previously turned it off,

Type: SHFT F8 (**FORMAT**)

Select: Option 1 (**LINE**)

Select: Option 3 (**JUSTIFIED**)

Response: No

Type: Y

Response: Yes

Any text you place in the column now will be justified. Extra spaces will be inserted between each word in order to achieve lines of equal length.

If, however, you've been working with justified type, and want to create flush-left/ragged-right columns,

Type: SHFT F8 (**FORMAT**)

Select: Option 1 (**LINE**)

Select: Option 3 (**JUSTIFIED**)

Response: Yes

Type: N

Response: No

Each word is separated by equal amounts of white space. As a result, each line will be a slightly different length. (As you'll see in Chapter Seven, you can regulate the amount of white space in the right-hand margin of each line by using Word-Perfect's **HYPHENATION** [SHFT F8, 1, 1] and **HYPHENA-TION ZONE** [SHFT F8, 1, 2] commands.)

92

Adding Vertical Rules between Columns

WordPerfect makes it easy to add vertical rules between columns. As described in Chapter Two, rules can be as thick or thin as you want and—depending upon your printer—you can add "color" to your document by shading rules to various gradations of gray.

Vertical rules between columns can extend the full height of the page or can be shortened to accommodate headlines or illustrations that span more than one column.

To add rules between the columns of your three-column document that will extend the full height of the page,

Type: ALT F9 (**GRAPHICS**)

Select: Option 5 (**LINE**)

Select: Option 2 (**VERTICAL LINE**)

Response: WordPerfect then displays the **VERTICAL LINE DRAW** menu.

Select: Option 1 (**HORIZONTAL POSITION**)

Select: Option 3 (**BETWEEN COLUMNS**)

Response: The first option to appear will be **Place Line To the Right of Column 1**. Accept this by entering (**RETURN**) (**RETURN**)

Type: ALT F9 (**GRAPHICS**)

Select: Option 5 (**LINE**)

Select: Option 2 (**VERTICAL LINE**)

Response: WordPerfect then displays the **VERTICAL LINE DRAW** menu.

Select: Option 1 (**HORIZONTAL POSITION**)

Select: Option 3 (**BETWEEN COLUMNS**)

Response: Place line to the Right of Column: 1.

Type: 2

Type: (RETURN)

Use WordPerfect's **VIEW DOCUMENT** command (SHFT F7, 6) to preview your work. You'll see that vertical rules extending the full height of each page have been accurately placed between the columns.

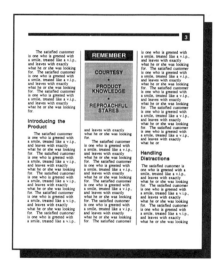

To shorten the lines so they won't interfere with a headline or illustration spanning more than one column,

Type: ALT F9 (**GRAPHICS**)

Select: Option 5 (**LINE**)

Select: Option 2 (**VERTICAL LINE**)

Response: WordPerfect then displays the **VERTICAL LINE DRAW** menu.

Select: Option 1 (**HORIZONTAL POSITION**)

Select: Option 3 (**BETWEEN COLUMNS**)

Response: The first option to appear is Place line to the Right of Column: 1   Accept this by entering (**RETURN**).

Select: Option 2 (**VERTICAL POSITION**)

Select: Option 4 (**BOTTOM**)

The line will extend up from the bottom of the page. To determine how high you want the line to extend,

Select: Option 3 (**LENGTH OF LINE**)

Response: 9" This is the normal default for a line that would extend the full height of the page. (Note, this number may be different, depending upon the particular page layout and your printer and monitor.)

Type: 6

Type: (RETURN)

That replaces the nine-inch default with a six-inch line. To place a six-inch vertical rule between columns two and three, again press (**RETURN**) (**RETURN**)

Type: ALT F9 (**GRAPHICS**)

Select: Option 5 (**LINE**)

Select: Option 2 (**VERTICAL LINE**)

Response: WordPerfect then displays the **VERTICAL LINE DRAW** menu.

Select: Option 1 (**HORIZONTAL POSITION**)

Select: Option 3 (**BETWEEN COLUMNS**)

Response: Place line to the Right of Column: 1.

Type: 2

Type: (RETURN)

That places the line between the second and third columns.

Again, the nine-inch default is replaced with a six-inch line.

When you **PRINT** (SHFT F7, 2) or **VIEW DOCUMENT** (SHFT F7, 6), you'll see that the six-inch vertical rules now extend between each of the columns of the page, leaving space for a large headline, horizontal illustration or scanned photograph.

Similar steps are used to place the rule between the first and second or second and third columns and extend it from the top of a page. To begin the rules at the top of a page and extend down to accommodate an illustration three inches high at the lower right,

Type: ALT F9 (**GRAPHICS**)

Select: Option 5 (**LINE**)

Select: Option 2 (**VERTICAL LINE**)

Response: WordPerfect then displays the **VERTICAL LINE DRAW** menu.

Select: Option 1 (**HORIZONTAL POSITION**)

Select: Option 3 (**BETWEEN COLUMNS**)

Response: The first option to appear is Place line to the Right of Column:1.

Type: Accept this by entering (**RETURN**) (**RETURN**). Notice that Option 2 (**VERTICAL POSITION**) default is **Full Page**.

Type: ALT F9 (**GRAPHICS**)

Select: Option 5 (**LINE**)

Select: Option 2 (**VERTICAL LINE**)

Response: WordPerfect then displays the **VERTICAL LINE DRAW** menu.

Select: Option 1 (**HORIZONTAL POSITION**)

Select: Option 3 (**BETWEEN COLUMNS**)

Response: Place line to right of column:1

Type: 2

Type: (RETURN)

WordPerfect now knows that you're defining the attributes of the rule between the second and third columns.

Select: Option 2 (**VERTICAL POSITION**)

Select: Option 2 (**TOP**)

The line now extends down from the top of the page.

To determine how far down you want the line to extend,

Select: Option 3 (**LENGTH OF LINE**)

Response: 0.16" This is the normal default for a line extending down from the top of a page.

Type: 6

Type: (RETURN) (RETURN)

That replaces the 0.16-inch default with a six-inch line.

When you **PRINT** (SHFT F7, 2) or **VIEW DOCUMENT** (SHFT F7, 6), your page should resemble the following illustration. There is now room for a two-column chart, graph, illustration or scanned photograph.

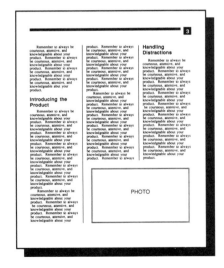

Using Column Display

When editing multi-column documents, you can work more efficiently if you take advantage of WordPerfect's **COLUMN DISPLAY** feature. It temporarily places each column on a separate page, which speeds up scrolling and screen rewriting (updating the screen each time text is entered or deleted).

To activate, or deactivate, WordPerfect's **COLUMN DISPLAY** feature,

Type: SHFT F1 (**SETUP**)

Select: Option 3 (**DISPLAY**)

Select: Option 8 (**SIDE-BY-SIDE COLUMNS DISPLAY**)

Response: Y

Accept the (**YES**) default if you want your screen to display columns side-by-side, as they're printed. Otherwise,

Select: N (**NO**)

That temporarily deactivates the side-by-side feature. Then you can concentrate on the contents of just one column at a time and enjoy faster editing and screen rewriting.

To verify your column setup, use **REVEAL CODES** (ALT F3), which provides a visual review of the width and placement of each column, the type of column you've selected and whether the **COLUMNS ON/OFF** command has been activated.

Using Macros to Speed Page Layout

It's entirely possible that you'll want to use more than one page layout structure for your projects. For example, you might want to have one column format for the introduction of your book, another format for the copy that follows and a third format for the index.

WordPerfect's macros make it easy to change from one column format to another. Assign a name to each column format (e.g.,

CHAPHDS, INTRO, TWOCOL, THREECOL, FOURCOL, etc.) and create a macro file (as described in Chapter Two) for each page format. (In Chapter Nine, you'll learn how to edit these macro files.)

Planning Your Documents

You can expedite the process of creating multi-column documents if you first make actual-size layouts of your pages using traditional design tools—i.e., a pencil, paper and ruler. Sketch the page layout you want to create, measure the placement and width of each column, and enter the correct numbers on WordPerfect's **TEXT COLUMN** definition screen.

Remember that unless your computer has a large screen monitor and enhanced graphics capabilities, you'll only be able to see your page layouts by using WordPerfect's **VIEW DOCUMENT** command (SHFT F7, 6)—or when you print out your project. So, the more planning you do, the faster your projects will proceed. More on this in Section Two.

Placing Headlines in Multi-column Documents

WordPerfect offers two ways to create headlines or nameplates that span one or more columns when you're working in a multi-column format. The method you choose depends upon the type of printer you use and the typeface, type size and style options available. Your choice also will be influenced by whether you intend to use other draw-type programs.

For example, as discussed in the Appendix, there will probably be times when you want to use a sophisticated drawing program to create a publication nameplate—or masthead—that will be repeated from issue to issue. A nameplate might include sophisticated text and graphics that are more efficiently created with a specialized drawing program than with WordPerfect. You might want to create your publication's masthead with a program such as PC Paintbrush, Windows Draw or Dr. Halo. They give you more power to adjust the precise location and shading of the various letters and integrate letters with illustrations (such as scanned images of your logo or corporate seal).

One way to create a headline that spans more than one column is to turn off WordPerfect's **COLUMN** feature.

Type: ALT F7 (**MATH/COLUMN**)

Select: Option 3 (**COLUMN ON/OFF**)

Headline text will stretch from the left-hand margin to the right-hand margin.

After you've entered the headline,

Type: ALT F7 (**MATH/COLUMNS**)

Select: Option 3 (**COLUMN ON/OFF**)

You'll be returned again to a multi-column format.

Headline Boxes

You also can use WordPerfect's **USER-DEFINED BOX** feature to create a headline box. First, if you're working in multi-column format, use WordPerfect's **MATH/COLUMN** command (ALT F7, 3) to return to a single-column format.

Then, using WordPerfect's **GRAPHICS** command (ALT F9), make a **USER-DEFINED BOX** (Option 4) that spans the column, or columns, in which the headline is to appear.

After creating the box, you either can enter the text or use the box as a container to import a headline or newsletter masthead file, previously created with a separate draw-type program. The advantage of using a **USER-DEFINED BOX** (Option 4) is that the headline won't be included in your document's list of tables, figures or text boxes when you use WordPerfect's **LIST GENERATION** command (ALT F5, 6).

However, if you use **TEXT BOX**es (Option 3) as containers for sidebars, they automatically will be listed—along with short quotations or other text features placed inside **TEXT BOX**es—when you use the **LIST GENERATION** command.

To use that feature, let's assume you've created a short five-paragraph sidebar that elaborates upon a point raised in a major article. The index will be based on the caption you use to introduce the **TEXT BOX** containing the sidebar. Let's say that file has been saved under the filename, **GOVERNOR**, with the caption, **Governor endorses increased federal spending**.

To place the sidebar in your document,

Type: ALT F9 (**GRAPHICS**)

Select: Option 3 (**TEXT BOX**)

Select: Option 1 (**CREATE**)

Select: Option 1 (**FILENAME**)

Type: GOVERNOR (The name of the previously saved text file.)

Response: **GOVERNOR** now appears next to the filename prompt.

Select: Option 2 (**CAPTION**)

Type: Governor endorses increased federal spending.

WordPerfect uses this caption when compiling a list of sidebars or other text features.

Note how the vertical dimension of the **TEXT BOX** has been stretched to accommodate the amount of text you've entered. That's particularly important, because if you're working in a multi-column format, the width of the **TEXT BOX** is determined by the column within which it's placed.

Press **(RETURN)** to get back to your editing screen. You then can evaluate your work by using either the **PRINT** (SHFT F7, 2) or **VIEW DOCUMENT** (SHFT F7, 6) command.

TIP: When creating **TEXT BOX**es, be sure you don't include more copy than can fit inside the **TEXT BOX**. Remember that space must be left below the sidebar for the caption.

In later chapters, you'll see how WordPerfect lets you modify the appearance of **TEXT BOX**es and edit their contents.

Using Horizontal Rules within Columns

When working in a multi-column format, remember that lines and boxes are limited to the size of the column within which they're created. If you want to create a line or box that extends beyond the boundaries of the current column, turn off WordPerfect's **MATH/COLUMNS** feature (ALT F7, 3) before you create the line or box.

This works to your benefit, however, if you're using horizontal rules to separate adjacent articles or topics within a column. These rules automatically will conform to the dimensions of your column.

Let's assume you're working in multi-column format and have just finished one article and are about to begin another. To create a strong horizontal rule that will clearly separate the two topics,

Type: Start by using your (**RETURN**) key to add some white space between the end of one article and the location of the horizontal rule.

Type: ALT F9 (**GRAPHICS**)

Select: Option 5 (**LINE**)

Select: Option 1 (**HORIZONTAL LINE**)

Select: Option 1 (**HORIZONTAL POSITION**)

Select: Option 4 (**BOTH LEFT AND RIGHT**)

Select: Option 3 (**WIDTH OF LINE**)

Response: 0.01"

Type: .05

Type: (RETURN)

This changes the default to a wider rule.

Press (**RETURN**) to return to your screen for editing. Use WordPerfect's **PRINT** (SHFT F7, 2) or **VIEW DOCUMENT** (SHFT F7, 6) command to verify that the rule has been placed correctly.

Remember to add one, or more, carriage returns to add white space below the rule before beginning work on the next article in the column.

Moving On

Now that you've surveyed WordPerfect's major page layout features, it's time to look at its ability to organize a publication. WordPerfect's organizing tools help readers quickly locate information—such as graphs, illustrations or data organized in tables.

As you'll see, WordPerfect 5.0 (and succeeding versions) offers document organizing power far beyond that offered by many popular conventional desktop publishing programs.

4

Document Organization

If you can't judge a book by its cover, you probably can judge it by its organizational features. A thorough table of contents and index allow readers to glean information quickly and efficiently. Yet, developing such tools can be an arduous task.

WordPerfect, however, has strong document organizational capabilities. As you write, edit or format your document, you can insert commands that automatically compile

- Table of contents
- Lists of subjects
- Lists of tables, charts and graphs
- Lists of illustrations and photographs
- Word index

By using these tools, regardless of the size of the book or training manual, readers quickly can locate the words or graphic information they need.

Creating a Table of Contents

WordPerfect's document organization features also make it easy to create a table of contents—perhaps positioned strategically on the front cover of your catalog, newsletter or formal report to entice readers.

Creating a table of contents involves more than just listing chapter headings and subheads. You also must design and generate it.

WordPerfect allows you to include as many as five levels of detail, which organize information into a hierarchy—ranging from "very important" to the "supporting detail" level. Readers in academic or technical fields, in particular, appreciate this format, which allows them to skim the table of contents to locate information quickly.

To create a table of contents, highlight the chapter titles and subheadings you want to include. Move the cursor to the first word in your first chapter title.

Type: ALT F4 (**BLOCK**)

Select: Using the left and right cursor control keys by themselves or in conjunction with **CTRL** (which advances the cursor one word at a time), highlight the first title you want included in your table of contents.

Type: ALT F5 (**MARK TEXT**)

Select: Option 1 (**ToC**)—**TABLE OF CONTENTS**

Response: ToC Level:

Type: 1, 2, 3, 4 or 5 (depending upon the priority of the highlighted information; one is the highest level, five is the lowest.)

TIP: Assign chapter headings to **Level 1**, subheadings to **Level 2** and secondary subheadings to **Level 3**.

Go through your entire document and mark all the words and phrases to be included in your table of contents.

Next, define the appearance of your table of contents. Place your cursor at the end of the page before the location of your table of contents.

Type: CTRL (RETURN) (**HARD PAGE**)

Type: Advance your cursor to the position where you want the table of contents to begin.

Type: The title of your table of contents. (Add extra space below the title, if you want.)

Type: ALT F5 (**MARK TEXT**)

Select: Option 5 (**DEFINE**)

Select: Option 1 (**DEFINE TABLE OF CONTENTS**)

Response: TABLE OF CONTENTS definition screen

```
Table of Contents Definition

   1 - Number of Levels                    1

   2 - Display Last Level in               No
       Wrapped Format

   3 - Page Numbering - Level 1            Flush right with leader
                        Level 2
                        Level 3
                        Level 4
                        Level 5




Selection: 0
```

Select: Option 1 (**NUMBER OF LEVELS**)

Type: 3 (if this is the level of detail you're including in your table of contents.)

Select: Option 2 (**DISPLAY LAST LEVEL IN WRAPPED FORMAT**) (if you're using the lowest level of detail and want long phrases continued from the right-hand end of one line to wrap around—or to be indented properly at the beginning of the next line. Otherwise, accept the **No** default.)

Select: Option 3 (**PAGE NUMBERING**) (unless you're willing to accept the default, **Flush Right with Leader** page number position.)

Response: You're offered several options for each of the table of contents levels you selected in Option 1 (**NUMBER OF LEVELS**):

Option 1 (**NONE**)
Option 2 (**PAGE # FOLLOWS**) without parentheses around the page number.
Option 3 (**(PAGE #) FOLLOWS**) with the page number in parentheses.
Option 4 (**FLUSH RT**) without a row of dots connecting the entry and the page number.
Option 5 (**FLUSH RT WITH LEADER**) with a row of dots, which helps the reader relate entries to page numbers.

Type: (RETURN) (if you accept the default page number position— **Flush Right with Leader** dots—for your table of contents.)

To generate your table of contents,

Type: ALT F5 (**MARK TEXT**)

Select: Option 6 (**GENERATE**)

Select: Option 5 (**GENERATE TABLES, INDEXES, AUTOMATIC REFERENCES**)

Response: Existing tables, lists and indexes will be replaced. Continue? (Y/N) Yes

Type: Y

Type: (RETURN)

The following table of contents appears:

Contents

Introduction

Section One: The Elements of Graphic Design

Chapter 1: Beginning Observations

Keeping Track of Drawings and Illustrations

As described in Chapter Two, illustrations and scanned photographs are added to WordPerfect documents by being placed in previously created **FIGURE, TABLE, TEXT** or **USER-DEFINED** graphics boxes. These boxes are numbered automatically as you create them and renumbered if you add or delete other boxes.

When creating these graphics boxes, WordPerfect prompts you to write a caption for each chart, graph, table, illustration or scanned image. These captions are the basis of compiled lists of illustrations and photographs, which form separate files that can be placed anywhere in your document. For example, a list of illustrations might appear at the front or back of your book or training manual.

TIP: Remember that WordPerfect compiles a list starting at the beginning of your document and working toward the end, where the list will appear. If you want a list to appear at the beginning of the document, follow the procedure outlined below to generate the list. Then use WordPerfect's **BLOCK** (ALT F4) and **MOVE** (CTRL F4, 2) commands to move the list from the end of your document to the beginning. To place your list on the page on which you want it, move the cursor to the desired position, use the **MOVE** command (CTRL F4, l) to retrieve the list. Then press (**RETURN**).

To generate a list of illustrations, place the cursor at the end of your document. At this point, use the (**RETURN**) key to add as much space as you want between the top of the page and the heading for your list.

Type: The heading you assign your list (e.g., **ILLUSTRATIONS**)

To center your heading, use WordPerfect's **CENTER** command (SHFT F6).

TIP: When entering headings, you can choose any available typeface, type size or type style by using WordPerfect's **FONT** command (CTRL F8) described in Chapter Six.
Next, select the type of list you want to generate.

Type: ALT F5 (**MARK TEXT**)

Response: List number (1 - 9):

Options 1 through 5 allow you to create lists based around whatever category of list you want to create. However, if you want your list based on captions created for **FIGURE, TABLE, TEXT** or **USER-DEFINED BOX**es, choose from Options 6 through 9.

Select Option 6 if you want to generate a list compiled from **FIGURE CAPTIONS**. Select Option 7 if you want to generate a list compiled from **TABLE CAPTIONS**. Select Option 8 if you want to generate a list compiled from **TEXT CAPTIONS**. Select Option 9 if you want to generate a list compiled from **USER-DEFINED BOX CAPTIONS**.

Type: 6 (**FIGURE CAPTIONS**)

Select: Choose from the following alternatives:

Option 1 (**NO PAGE NUMBERS)**
Option 2 (**PAGE NUMBERS FOLLOW ENTRIES)**
Option 3 (**PAGE NUMBERS) FOLLOW ENTRIES**
Option 4 (**FLUSH RIGHT PAGE NUMBERS)**
Option 5 (**FLUSH RIGHT PAGE NUMBERS WITH LEADERS)**

Finally, generate the list.

Type: ALT F5 (**MARK TEXT)**

Select: Option 6 (**GENERATE)**

Select: Option 5 (**GENERATE TABLES, INDEXES, AUTOMATIC REFERENCES)**

Response: Existing tables, lists and indexes will be replaced. Continue? (Y/N) Yes

Type: Y

Type: (RETURN)

The following is a typical **FIGURE LIST** that can be placed either at the front of a book or training manual.

ILLUSTRATIONS

Figure 1. Map of Poland - 1945

Figure 2. Map of Russia - 1980

Figure 3. Diagram of Battle Fields

Figure 4. Map of Separation

Figure 5. Map of Italy - 1966

Figure 6. Diagram of Truck Routes

Figure 7. Map of Italy - 1940

Figure 8. Map of Europe - 1980

Keeping Track of Tables, Charts and Graphs

Regardless of whether you're producing a book, financial proposal or formal report, lists of tables, charts and graphs add further credibility to your document and help readers quickly inventory and locate information. Many readers will want to go directly to the pages containing the tables, charts and graphs that provide concise, visual displays of important numbers.

To create these lists, you use a procedure similar to the one used to compile lists of illustrations. Follow the same process of defining the location and appearance of a file that is assembled automatically, based on the captions you added when creating **TABLE BOX**es. To compile a list of **TABLE BOX**es.

Select: Option 7 (**TABLE BOXES**)

When making your choice, remember the following:

Option 6 creates a list of **FIGURE BOX**es
Option 7 creates a list of **TABLE BOX**es
Option 8 creates a list of **TEXT BOX**es
Option 9 creates a list of **USER-DEFINED BOX**es

Keeping Track of Sidebars and Articles

If your publication includes numerous short articles or features, WordPerfect's ability to keep track of **TEXT BOX**es can be of value. For example, you might use **TEXT BOX**es for sidebars—short articles that elaborate upon information contained in the body copy of a book or newsletter.

You also can use WordPerfect's ability to create an index of **TEXT BOX**es to identify departments within a newsletter (e.g., a calendar of events, or a list of recent promotions, awards and outstanding accomplishments).

You even can create a list based on WordPerfect's **USER-DEFINED BOX**es, which add flexibility by letting you create lists of more than one type of **TEXT BOX.**

TIP: If you create a box and don't give it a caption, it won't be included in a compiled list. The **FIGURE, TABLE, TEXT** or **USER-DEFINED BOX NUMBER** will be omitted from the list, which can be quite noticeable.

Creating an Index

You can create a subject index by *marking* text (highlighting words or phrases as they appear in your document). You then can generate a list by using WordPerfect's **LIST GENERATE** command (ALT F5, 6, 5).

While writing or editing your document, locate and highlight each word or phrase you want included in the index. If you want to include multiple word entries in your index, use WordPerfect's **BLOCK** command (ALT F4) and the cursor control keys to highlight the words or phrases you want to include. Remember that you quickly can advance the cursor one word at a time by using **CTRL** plus the left or right cursor control keys.

Type: ALT F4 (**BLOCK**)

Type: Use the cursor control keys to extend the highlighting through the entire word.

Type: ALT F5 (**MARK TEXT**)

Select: Option 3 (**INDEX**)

Response: Index Heading: (and the word or words you've highlighted.)

If you want to accept the word or phrase as it stands, press (**RETURN**). If, however, you want to use a different word or phrase summarizing the highlighted word or phrase,

Type: The words that summarize the word or phrase you want added to your index.

When you've finished,

Type: (RETURN)

Response: Subheading: (and the word or phrase you've highlighted.)

If you don't want to include a subheading in your index,

Type: Spacebar

Type: (RETURN)

If you want a subheading, type in the words that describe the original highlighted word or phrase. Then press (**RETURN**).

When you've marked all the words and phrases you want to include, you can generate the index. Start by placing your cursor where you want the index to appear in your document.

Type: ALT F5 (**MARK TEXT**)

Select: Option 3 (**INDEX**)

Response: Index Heading

Type: The title of your index.

Next, you must define the appearance of the index. Move the cursor to the end of your document, and start a new page.

Type: CTRL (RETURN) (**HARD PAGE**)

Type: Enter a title for the index. (Add any extra spaces you might want between the title and the references.)

Type: ALT F5 (**MARK TEXT**)

Select: Option 5 (**DEFINE**)

Select: Option 3 (**DEFINE INDEX**)

Next, select a numbering style for your index.

Select: Choose one of the following five alternatives:

Option 1 (**NO PAGE NUMBERS**)
Option 2 (**PAGE NUMBERS FOLLOW ENTRIES**)
Option 3 (**PAGE NUMBERS**) FOLLOW ENTRIES
Option 4 (**FLUSH RIGHT PAGE NUMBERS**)
Option 5 (**FLUSH RIGHT PAGE NUMBER WITH LEADERS**)

Now, generate the index.

Type: ALT F5 (**MARK TEXT**)

Select: Option 6 (**GENERATE**)

Select: Option 5 (**GENERATE TABLES, INDEXES, AUTOMATIC REFERENCES**)

Response: Existing tables, lists and indexes will be replaced. Continue? (Y/N) Yes

Type: Y

Type: (RETURN)

Working with a Concordance File

A concordance file simplifies and expedites the process of creating an index. It's used when a word or phrase appears frequently in your document. After a word is added to a concordance file, WordPerfect automatically searches and adds other occurrences of that word to your index, saving you a lot of time.

To create a concordance file, you must let WordPerfect know which words or phrases you want it to find automatically.

Type: SHFT F3 (**SWITCH**)

Type: The words you want WordPerfect to search.

Type: F7 (**EXIT**)

Response: Save document? Y/N (Yes)

117

Type: Y or (RETURN)

Response: Document to be saved:

Type: An easily remembered name for the concordance file. (**CONCORDA** comes to mind.)

Type: (RETURN)

Be sure to erase this file after you've used it to compile the index for a particular project. Alternately, if you're working on more than one project at a time, you could name your concordance files **1CONCORD**, **2CONCORD**, **3CONCORD**, etc.

After you've saved your concordance file, you're prompted to return to your main document.

Response: Exit doc 2? (Y/N) No

Type: Y

Alternately, you can return to your main document by using WordPerfect's **SWITCH** command (SHFT F3).

Creating an Index with a Concordance File

To create an index that includes a concordance file, enter the name of the concordance file when you define the index.

Type: ALT F5 (**MARK TEXT**)

Select: Option 5 (**DEFINE**)

Select: Option 3 (**DEFINE INDEX**)

Response: Concordance Filename (Enter=none):

Type: CONCORDA (or the filename you've chosen.)

Type: (RETURN)

Select: The page number definition you want, as described above.

To generate the list,

Type: ALT F5 (**MARK TEXT**)

Select: Option 6 (**GENERATE**)

Select: Option 5 (**GENERATE TABLES, INDEXES, AUTOMATIC REFERENCES**)

Response: Existing tables, lists and indexes will be replaced. Continue? (Y/N) Yes

Type: (RETURN)

When completed, every word listed in the concordance file is listed automatically in the index, with every page number indicating where a word or phrase is found.

TIP: While writing and editing, try to be as consistent as possible in using singular and plural versions of the same word. If both are included in your manuscript, remember to include them in your concordance file. Unassisted, WordPerfect doesn't know that "books" is the plural of "book," etc.

Footnotes and Endnotes

WordPerfect's document-organizing features also make it easy to provide readers with ancillary information in footnotes and endnotes to further strengthen your message.

To create a **FOOTNOTE** or **ENDNOTE**, locate the cursor to the position where you want the note number inserted. When your cursor is located next to the word or phrase you want amplified,

Type: CTRL F7 (**FOOTNOTE**)

Select: Choose one of the following options:

Option 1 (**FOOTNOTE**) if you want the supporting material to be included on the same page as the reference.

Option 2 (**ENDNOTE**) if you want the supporting material to be gathered together at the end of your document.

Select: Option 1 (**CREATE**)

Type: Enter the words you want included in either your footnote or endnote.

Type: F7 (**EXIT**) (when you've finished entering the text.)

TIP: Use WordPerfect's **FONT** command (CTRL F8) if you want footnotes or endnotes to appear with a different typeface, type size, type style or line spacing from the body copy of your document. Remember that **FONT** choices must be entered before the footnote number.

Editing Footnotes and Endnotes

You can edit footnotes and endnotes at any point.

Type: CTRL F7 (**FOOTNOTE**)

Select: Option 1 (**FOOTNOTES**)
or
Option 2 (**ENDNOTES**)

Select: Option 2 (**EDIT**)

Response: Footnote number? 1 (The number that appears is the number of the last footnote created.)

Type: The number of the footnote or endnote you want to edit.

Type: (RETURN)

Renumbering Footnotes and Endnotes

You can renumber footnotes and endnotes at any point (e.g., when you start a new chapter or section of a book or training manual). Using the above example, select **CTRL 7**, Option 1 or **2**. Then choose **NEW NUMBER** (Option 3). WordPerfect asks you which number to begin with and then assigns it to the next footnote or endnote you create.

Automatic References

Often when creating books and training materials, you'll want to refer the reader to topics covered in greater detail at a later point. Or, you might want to refer the reader to illustrations, graphs or numeric tables in later chapters. WordPerfect's **AUTOMATIC REFERENCE** feature lets you forward reference—even if you don't know the exact location of the upcoming reference. WordPerfect keeps track of the correct upcoming page. It automatically updates and renumbers the page reference if words, paragraphs or pages are added or deleted.

Likewise, it updates the box number if you forward reference a specific **FIGURE** or **TABLE BOX** as intervening boxes are added or deleted (e.g., "See Figure 31, Population Changes 1900-1950").

WordPerfect can even create multiple references that list both box numbers and page numbers: "See Figure 31, Population Changes, 1900-1950, Page 149."

Generating Automatic References

By automatically creating forward references, WordPerfect can save you a lot of time. If a reader is impatient to learn more about a subject, or how you arrived at a conclusion, a forward reference lets the reader jump to the page containing the information he or she wants.

To create a forward reference,

Type: Begin by typing an introductory phrase, such as **See Population Growth, page**, and add a space.

Type: ALT F5 (**MARK TEXT**)

Select: Option 6 (**GENERATE**)

Select: Option 5 (**GENERATE TABLES, INDEXES, AUTOMATIC REFERENCES**)

Response: Existing tables, lists and indexes are replaced. Continue? (Y/N) Yes.

Type: N

You're returned to the editing screen. Place your cursor where you want the page reference to appear.

Type: ALT F5 (**MARK TEXT**)

Select: Option 1 (**AUTOMATIC REFERENCE**)

Select: Option 3 (**MARK BOTH REFERENCE AND TARGET**) (if you know the location of your forward reference.)

Select: Choose from the following types of references:

Option 1 (**PAGE NUMBER**)
Option 2 (**PARAGRAPH/OUTLINE NUMBER**)
Option 3 (**FOOTNOTE NUMBER**)
Option 4 (**ENDNOTE NUMBER**)
Option 5 (**GRAPHICS BOX NUMBER**)

Type: Advance the cursor to the word or graphics box on the page to which you want to refer the reader.

Type: (RETURN)

Response: Target name

Type: Enter a word that identifies the reference, or highlight the word by using WordPerfect's **BLOCK** command (ALT F4 and the cursor control keys).

Type: (RETURN)

TIP: Incomplete references are indicated by a question mark on your screen. They remind you that you haven't defined a target location. Use WordPerfect's **SEARCH** command (F2) to locate incomplete references quickly.

Updating References

You should update your **AUTOMATIC REFERENCE**s frequently, particularly before printing.

To update an **AUTOMATIC REFERENCE** list,

Type: ALT F5 (**MARK TEXT**)

Select: Option 6 (**GENERATE**)

Select: Option 5 (**GENERATE TABLES, INDEXES, AUTOMATIC REFERENCES**)

Response: Existing tables, lists and indexes will be replaced. Continue? (Y/N) Yes

Type: (RETURN) (to accept the default.)

Creating Master Documents

As you begin to create more ambitious desktop publishing projects, such as books or training manuals, your working files will become larger and larger. That can slow down document editing because numerous pages must be repaginated every time you enter or delete a word or paragraph. In addition, **FIGURE, TEXT** and other boxes, as well as footnotes and endnotes, have to be renumbered when you add or delete boxes or notes.

Large files also slow down the spell-check process, as you're forced to recheck pages (unless you confine spell-checking to just one page at a time).

However, WordPerfect's **MASTER DOCUMENT** feature ensures that editing and spell-checking will clip along at a fast pace. With it, you can create a relatively small master document that includes numerous subdocuments—such as individual chapters in a book.

To create a master document that will organize a series of individual files, open a new file. Then,

Type: ALT F5 (**MARK TEXT**)

Select: Option 2 (**SUBDOC**)

Type: Enter the name of the document file and any additional text or subdocuments you want to include.

Type: F10 (**SAVE**) (when you're finished.)

TIP: Be sure to give your master document an easily identifiable filename, so you won't have trouble locating it at a later date. The name should differ dramatically from subdocument filenames (e.g., **WPBOOK,** instead of **CHAP1** or **CHAP2**, etc).

Generating a Master Document

A master document has to be expanded before you can edit or print it. To expand it,

Type: ALT F5 (**MARK TEXT**)

Select: Option 6 (**GENERATE**)

Select: Option 3 (**EXPAND MASTER DOCUMENT**)

Because a single, large file is created out of several individual files, expanding a master document can take several minutes.

As this is occurring, pages are being renumbered, as are footnotes, endnotes and lists of **FIGURE**, **TEXT**, **TABLE** and **USER-DEFINED BOX**es.

TIPS: 1) Because of the time spent expanding your master document, you should save it immediately after expanding it. 2) Remember that tables of contents, footnotes, endnotes, indexes and lists of boxes are recompiled and renumbered when master documents are created.

Condensing a Master Document

To return to a smaller, more manageable master file,

Type: (HOME) (HOME) Up Cursor Control Key

Type: ALT F5 (**MARK TEXT**)

Select: Option 6 (**GENERATE**)

Select: Option 4 (**CONDENSE MASTER DOCUMENT**)

Response: Save Subdocs? (Y/N) Yes

Type: (RETURN) (to accept the default.)

Response: Replace (Subdoc 1)?
1. Yes; 2. No; 3. Replace All Remaining.

Select: 3

Response: Replace All Remaining.

With Option 3, all subdocuments will be saved with any editing changes you've made. Option 1 lets you save subdocuments one by one. Option 2 doesn't save editing changes.

Moving On

You're now familiar with the ways WordPerfect helps you organize your documents by compiling lists of **FIGURE**, **TABLE**, **TEXT** and **USER-DEFINED BOX**es as well as creating tables of contents, indexes and forward references.

The following two chapters focus on manipulating graphics and text—the foundation of graphic design. You'll learn ways in which WordPerfect lets you manipulate them to improve the appearance of your documents, as well as increase readability.

You'll learn how to expedite document assembly by creating sophisticated macros and **STYLE**s. You'll be introduced to the WordPerfect Library software program and see how it can further improve your productivity.

5

The Graphics Connection

As described in Chapter Two, charts, graphs, illustrations and scanned photographs created with other software programs are placed in WordPerfect documents by using boxes—**TEXT, FIGURE, TABLE** and **USER-DEFINED BOX**es. These boxes smoothly integrate text and graphics into good-looking, effective print communications.

Even after they've been created, boxes offer a lot of design flexibility. They can be enlarged or reduced in size or moved to a different position. Box borders can be changed, and backgrounds screened. In addition, caption placement can be adjusted, as can the amount of white space between a box and its text, or surrounding a box.

WordPerfect gives you total control over the content of boxes. You can move, resize, rotate or even create reversal effects with graphic images.

Imported graphics, for example, can be cropped by moving them within their box.

Likewise, imported graphic images can be increased or decreased in size:

What Are Graphics?

Illustrations and scanned photographs are the most frequently used types of graphics. Illustrations can be created with either draw-type or paint-type (bit-map) programs.

Paint-type programs define the placement of individual dots—called pixels. They offer less latitude for image enlargement or reduction. When the images are reduced in size, the dots become too close to each other and detail is lost. Likewise, enlargement can cause an image to break up, because the dots defining the image are moved farther apart.

Photographs can be scanned. Some programs even allow you to hook up a home video camera to your computer and capture "live" images.

Software programs that create graphics files which can be directly placed in WordPerfect documents (partial list):

- AutoCAD
- Dr. Halo II
- GEM Paint
- GEM SCAN
- Lotus 1-2-3
- Lotus Symphony
- Macintosh Paint
- PC Paint Plus
- PC Paintbrush
- PFS: Professional Plan
- Microsoft Windows Paint

Software programs that create graphics files which can be placed in WordPerfect documents after conversion to a compatible file format (partial list):

- Adobe Illustrator
- Boeing Graph
- ChartMaster
- Harvard Graphics
- HP Scanning Gallery
- SuperCalc4
- VP Planner

Graphic images also include charts and graphs created with popular spreadsheet programs, such as Lotus 1-2-3, Microsoft Excel, WordPerfect's PlanPerfect, Computer Associates' SuperCalc4 and other programs that convert the results of financial computation and analysis into strong visual statements.

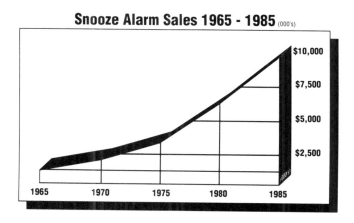

Snooze Alarm Sales 1965 - 1985 (000's)

It's important to note, however, that there's more to graphics than illustrations, scanned photographs, graphs and charts. Words also can be "graphics."

For example, you can create a sophisticated masthead as a WordPerfect file, and import and resize it as needed. You might use a sophisticated drawing-type program to create a distinctive nameplate—or masthead—for a magazine or newsletter. You might even hire an outside graphic artist to create a masthead file using a highly sophisticated drawing program you wouldn't normally need on a day-to-day basis.

Or, you might use a scanner to copy your firm's logo, so it easily can be placed in your advertisements, brochures and newsletters. Once your logo has been scanned, you can use it over and over again at various sizes in different documents.

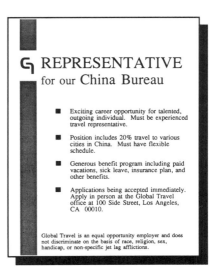

Modifying Figure Boxes

After you've created a box, you may want to change its size or location. Your decision may be based on aesthetic considerations. A box might be so large that it overwhelms the page, or so small that it crowds the image it contains.

Another reason to change the size of a box relates to establishing a hierarchy of importance. Important graphics should be larger than supporting graphics. After laying out your publication, you might decide that certain charts, graphs, illustrations or scanned photographs deserve more emphasis. Therefore, they should be larger than the other images.

You might want to change the size and location of boxes when a page contains two or more charts, graphs or illustrations. Strong page design often features boxes of different sizes, adding contrast and increasing visual interest.

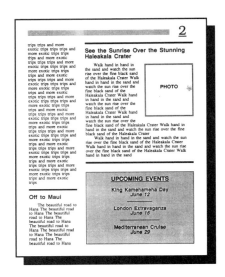

As an example of the ease with which you can change the location and dimensions of a box, start by recreating the **FIGURE BOX** containing the **CLOCK.WPG** file used in Chapter Two.

TIP: Although you'll use **FIGURE BOX** in the following illustrations, remember that many of the same command options also work with **TABLE, TEXT** and **USER-DEFINED BOX**es. Remember that each type of box can contain text or graphics. The different box categories primarily exist so WordPerfect can generate different types of lists after your document has been completed. For example, it can compile a list of illustrations, if all illustrations have been placed in **FIGURE BOX**es. Or it can compile a list of charts, if all charts have been placed in **TABLE BOX**es.

Let's start by modifying a **FIGURE BOX**. Place the clock graphic used in Chapter Two into your document.

Type: ALT F9 (**GRAPHICS**)

Select: Option 1 (**FIGURE**)

Select: Option 1 (**CREATE**)

Response: GRAPHICS definition screen

```
Definition: Figure
      1 - Filename
      2 - Caption
      3 - Type                   Paragraph
      4 - Vertical Position      8"
      5 - Horizontal Position    Right
      6 - Size                   3.25" wide x 3.25" (high)
      7 - Wrap Text Around Box   Yes
      8 - Edit



Selection: 8
```

Select: Option 1 (**FILENAME**)

Type: CLOCK.WPG

Select: Option 3 (**TYPE**)

Select: Option 2 (**PAGE**)

Type: (RETURN)

Type: (RETURN)

This accepts all of the defaults. The result is a three-and-one-quarter-inch square **FIGURE BOX** placed in the upper right-hand corner of the page, if your cursor was located there when you created the box.

Use WordPerfect's **VIEW DOCUMENT** command (SHFT F7, 6) to preview the box; then **PRINT** (SHFT F7, 2), so that you can compare it with the example created below.

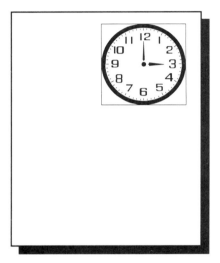

TIP: Always include **.WPG**, or the appropriate file ending, when importing graphics. Otherwise, the file cannot be placed in your document.

Remember to include DOS **PATH** commands in the filename. Otherwise, WordPerfect won't know which subdirectory contains the file you want to import.

Graphics files are usually stored in the same subdirectories as the software programs used to create them, unless you specify otherwise. For example, Lotus 1-2-3 and PlanPerfect charts and graphs are created in their respective Lotus 1-2-3 and PlanPerfect subdirectories. Publisher's Paintbrush files are created in the subdirectory containing the Publisher's Paintbrush program, etc.

WordPerfect can't read your mind. It can't search for a specific file located somewhere in your hard disk. As a result, you must specify the subdirectory in which the graphics file you want to import is stored. Alternately, before assembling your document, copy the files containing graphics files to the Word-Perfect 5.0 subdirectory.

Moving a Figure Box

To change the location of the clock on the page,

Type:　ALT F9 (**GRAPHICS**)

Select:　Option 1 (**FIGURE**)

Select:　Option 2 (**EDIT**)

Response:　Figure Number? 2 (Or one number higher than the last box created.)

Type:　1

Type:　(RETURN)

Response:　The original FIGURE definition screen appears.

```
Definition: Figure

       1 - Filename              CLOCK.WPG (Graphic)

       2 - Caption

       3 - Type                  Page

       4 - Vertical Position     Top

       5 - Horizontal Position   Margin, Right

       6 - Size                  3.25" wide x 3.25" (high)

       7 - Wrap Text Around Box  Yes

       8 - Edit




Selection: 8
```

To lower the box on the page,

Select: Option 4 (**VERTICAL POSITION**)

Response: You'll be offered the following options:

Option 1 (**FULL PAGE**)
Option 2 (**TOP**)
Option 3 (**CENTER**)
Option 4 (**BOTTOM**)
Option 5 (**SET POSITION**)

Select: Option 5 (**SET POSITION**)

Response: Offset from top of page 1.16"

Type: 3

Type: (RETURN)

Response: The graphics box is moved three inches down from the top of the page.

Type: (RETURN) (RETURN)

Response: This returns you to the editing screen and you can use **VIEW DOCUMENT** (SHFT F7, 6) to preview your page.

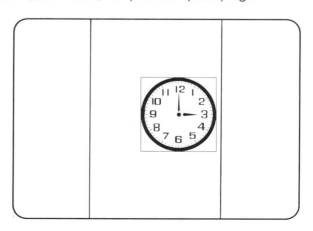

Now, let's move the graphic to the left.

Type: ALT F9 (**GRAPHICS**)

Select: Option 1 (**FIGURE**)

Select: Option 2 (**EDIT**)

Response: Figure 2

Type: 1

Type: (RETURN)

Again, replace the **FIGURE 2** default with **FIGURE 1**. When the original screen setup appears,

Select: Option 5 (**HORIZONTAL POSITION**)

Response: You'll be offered the following choices:

Option 1 (**MARGINS**)
Option 2 (**COLUMNS**)
Option 3 (**SET POSITION**)

Select: Option 3 (**SET POSITION**)

Response: Offset from left of page: 0"

Type: 3

Type: (RETURN) (RETURN)

The clock now is three inches from the left-hand border of the page in which it has been placed. Again, **VIEW DOCUMENT** (SHFT F7, 6) or **PRINT** (SHFT F7, 1).

By letting you align boxes with the borders of a page or column, WordPerfect makes it easy for you to control the appearance of your documents.

Other Placement Options

As described in Chapter Two, WordPerfect lets you define boxes as page-, paragraph- or character-locked. A page-locked box, such as the one used in the illustration above, is locked to a specific position on a page regardless of changes in the text surrounding it. Paragraph- and character-locked boxes, however, are placed with specific text surrounding them and will change page position as the position of the text changes.

Remember that the original vertical and horizontal position of paragraph-locked boxes is determined by cursor placement. By selecting Option 4 (**VERTICAL POSITION**) and/or Option 5 (**HORIZONTAL POSITION**), you can center the box on the page or within a column, or place it anywhere on the page. Choose from the following **VERTICAL POSITION** options:

Option 1 (**FULL PAGE**)
Option 2 (**TOP**)
Option 3 (**CENTER**)
Option 4 (**BOTTOM**)
Option 5 (**SET POSITION**)

HORIZONTAL POSITION options include:

Option 1 (**MARGINS**)
Option 2 (**COLUMNS**)
Option 3 (**SET POSITION**)

In both cases, **SET POSITION** lets you define the position of the box with mathematical accuracy. As you produce more sophisticated projects, you're likely to use the **HORIZONTAL** and **VERTICAL POSITION** options more and more.

TIP: You can change the measuring system at any point by executing WordPerfect's **SETUP** (SHFT F1, 8) command. You can specify cursor location in inches, points, centimeters or the column/cursor position measuring system used in previous versions of WordPerfect.

Type: SHFT F1 (**SETUP**)

Select: Option 8 (**UNITS OF MEASURE**)

You can choose between the following options:

    " for inches
    i for inches
    c for centimeters
    p for points

You also can choose Option **u** (for lines and columns), which is similar to the way WordPerfect 4.2 kept track of cursor location.

Resizing Figure Boxes

Not only is it easy to reposition boxes, it's also easy to enlarge or reduce them. Let's change the size of the **FIGURE BOX**:

Type: ALT F9 (**GRAPHICS**)

Select: Option 1 (**FIGURE**)

Select: Option 2 (**EDIT**)

Response: Figure 2 (or one number higher than the highest number created.)

Type: 1

Type: (RETURN)

This replaces the default **FIGURE 2** with **FIGURE 1**. When the original screen setup appears,

Select: Option 6 (**SIZE**)

Response: You're presented with three options:

    Option 1 (**WIDTH (AUTO HEIGHT)**)
    Option 2 (**HEIGHT (AUTO WIDTH)**)
    Option 3 (**BOTH WIDTH AND HEIGHT**)

If you choose Option 1 (**WIDTH (AUTO HEIGHT)**), the height of the box automatically will be made proportionate to the width of the graphics file being placed.

139

If you choose Option 2 (**HEIGHT (AUTO WIDTH)**), the width of the box automatically will be made proportionate to the height of the graphics file being introduced.

Option 3 (**BOTH WIDTH AND HEIGHT**) offers the most flexibility. You can arbitrarily determine the size of the box. You can distort the graphic by stretching or compressing it.

Proportionately Increasing Box Width

Let's make the box wider, but maintain correct proportions. Continuing from the three options presented above,

Select: Option 1 (**WIDTH (AUTO HEIGHT)**)

Response: Width = 3.25"

Type: 5

Type: (RETURN)

Response: Notice that because **CLOCK.WPG** is a square graphic, the height also is made five inches. If the original graphic were a rectangle, the height would increase by an amount proportionate to the width.

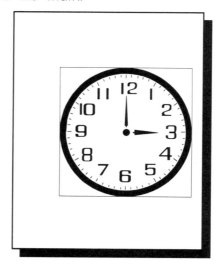

Proportionately Increasing Box Height

Next, let's proportionately reduce box size.

Select: Option 6 (**SIZE**)

Select: Option 2 (**HEIGHT (AUTO WIDTH)**)

Response: Height = 6"

Type: 2

Type: (RETURN)

Response: Notice how the width is reduced to 1.99 inches, again maintaining the correct proportions of the square graphic. (The 1.99 indicates the extreme accuracy with which Word-Perfect keeps track of box sizes.)

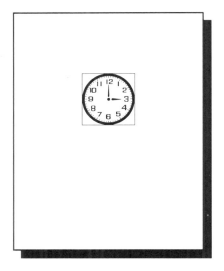

Now, create a rectangular box for the square graphic. Working with the same figure you just modified,

Select:	Option 6 (**SIZE**)
Select:	Option 3 (**BOTH HEIGHT AND WIDTH**)
Response:	Width = 1.99
Type:	5
Type:	(RETURN)
Response:	Height = 1.99"
Type:	4
Type:	(RETURN)

When you **VIEW DOCUMENT** (SHFT F7, 6) or **PRINT** (SHFT F7, 1), the clock will be centered in the box.

TIP: If you're using a Hewlett-Packard LaserJet II printer, remember that the maximum size of graphic images you can print is determined by the amount of printer memory. If you exceed memory limitations, graphic images will be printed on separate pieces of paper.

Creating Empty Figure Boxes

WordPerfect lets you create empty **FIGURE BOX**es before you create the files that will be placed in them. You can define their position and size, and place the graphics files in them later. To create empty **FIGURE BOX**es, leave Option 1 (**FILENAME**) blank.

Type: ALT F9 (**GRAPHICS**)

Select: Option 1 (**FIGURE**)

Select: Option 1 (**CREATE**)

Leave Option 1 (**FILENAME**) blank, and enter the **TYPE, VERTICAL POSITION, HORIZONTAL POSITION** and **SIZE** placement and dimensions desired. (**RETURN**) after you've defined the size and position.

Filling Empty Figure Boxes

Later you can return to the empty **FIGURE BOX** and place a graphics file.

Type: ALT F9 (**GRAPHICS**)

Select: Option 1 (**FIGURE**)

Select: Option 2 (**EDIT**)

Response: A new figure number (one higher than the number of the last **FIGURE BOX** you created) will be assigned.

Type: The number of the **FIGURE BOX** you want to fill.

Select:	Option 1 (**FILENAME**)
Type:	The name of the graphics file you want to insert. In this case, **ARROW1.WPG.**
Type:	(RETURN) (RETURN)
	Note that when you **VIEW DOCUMENT** (SHFT F7, 6) or **PRINT** (SHFT F7, 1) the box automatically will be resized to accommodate the graphics file you've imported.

Moving Graphics inside Boxes

You also can change the vertical or horizontal location of a graphic inside a box. This is similar to the way photographs are cropped, eliminating distracting details on the edges.

Type:	ALT F9 (**GRAPHICS**)
Select:	Option 1 (**FIGURE**)
Select:	Option 2 (**EDIT**)
Response:	Figure 2 (WordPerfect defaults to highest figure created.)
Type:	1
Type:	(RETURN) (to choose **FIGURE 1**.)
Select:	Option 8 (**EDIT**)
Response:	Figure 1, with the clock graphic, now appears on the screen.
Type:	Left cursor control key

Response: Each time you hit the left cursor control key, the clock will move slightly to the left, shifting by the percentage indicated in the lower right-hand corner of the screen. The default is 10 percent.

Type: (INSERT) (This changes the amount of displacement. You can choose 1, 5, 10 or 25 percent displacement.)

You also can move the graphic a specific distance.

Select: 1 (**MOVE**)

Response: Horizontal = 1"

Type: 2

Type: (RETURN) (RETURN)

This moves the clock two inches to the right.

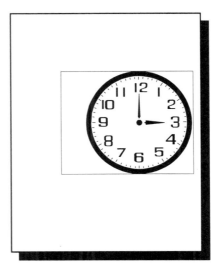

If you want to move the clock two inches to the left, enter a negative number (e.g., **-2**).

Response: Vertical = 1"

Type: 1.5

Type: (RETURN)

This moves the clock image one and a half inches higher in the box.

If you want to lower the clock one and a half inches, enter a negative number (e.g., **-1.5**).

Remember, positive numbers move the graphic image up and/or to the right. Negative numbers move the graphic down and/or to the left.

Resizing Graphic Images within Boxes

While in the **GRAPHICS EDIT** mode, you also can increase or decrease the size of the graphic image without changing the size of the box. Graphic images can be enlarged or reduced to emphasize important parts or eliminate unnecessary details at the edges.

Type: (PAGE UP)

Response: The clock is increased in size proportionate to the percentage indicated in the lower right-hand corner of your screen.

To reduce the size of the clock,

Type: (PAGE DOWN)

Response: The clock is decreased in size proportionate to the percentage indicated in the lower right-hand corner of your screen.

To change the percentage of enlargement or reduction,

Type: (INSERT)

Again, you can increase or decrease image size 1, 5, 10 or 25 percent by toggling the (**INSERT**) key.

You'll find that WordPerfect's **MOVE** and **SCALE** capabilities greatly improve the appearance of your projects by letting you place the graphics exactly where you want them, scaled to the size you want.

Creating Special Effects with Distorted Images

WordPerfect allows you to create special effects by distorting a graphic—disproportionately modifying the height and width of the image. While in the **EDIT** mode,

Select: Option 2 (**SCALE**)

Response: Scale X: 100

147

Type: 150

Type: (RETURN)

Response: Scale Y: 100

Type: 300

Type: (RETURN)

The result is a seriously distorted clock!

Returning to Your Original Graphic Image

After experimenting with moving and resizing the clock graphic, you may wish there were an easy way to return to the original clock image. WordPerfect provides one.

Type: CTRL (HOME) (**GO TO**)

Response: Instantly, the graphic returns to its original image.

Rotating Graphic Images

You also can rotate imported graphic images. To rotate the clock to the left,

Type: + (The gray plus key)

To rotate the clock to the right,

Type: - (The gray minus key)

Once again, you can control the degree of rotation by using the (**INSERT**) key to toggle between 1, 5, 10 and 25 percent image rotation.

Alternately, you can rotate the graphic image a specific number of degrees. To do this,

Select: Option 3 (**ROTATE**)

Response: Enter number of degrees (0-360): 0

Type: 90

Type: (RETURN)

Response: Mirror image? (Y/N) No

Type: (RETURN)

Response: The clock is rotated 90 degrees to the left (or counter-clockwise).

TIP: You only can rotate a graphic image once from its original position. For example, if you want to rotate an image 90 degrees, you must rotate it in one step, rather than in two separate 45-degree incremental steps.

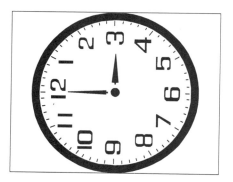

If, you want a mirror image, at the above prompt,

Type: Y

Response: The clock is rotated 90 degrees and appears to have a mirror image.

Again, you can restore the original graphic image by using WordPerfect's **GO TO** command (CTRL HOME).

Reversed Images

While editing bit-mapped graphic images, you can create negative, or reversal, effects. Bit-mapped graphic images are created with paint-type drawing programs and certain image scanners which let you create illustrations with a lot of shadow effects and varying shades of gray.

Reversed images can be used to create artistic, impressionistic effects. When you reverse a bit-mapped image, the white areas become black, and the black areas become white. The shape of the original illustration or scanned image remains recognizable, but more abstract and stylized. To reverse an image, continue to use the clock image.

Select: Option 4 (**INVERT**)

Note that this command has no effect upon draw-type images. It's primarily used with scanned photographs and illustrations.

In all of the above cases, WordPerfect's graphics power lets you manipulate boxes and graphic images until their proportions are exactly "right" for their environment.

Changing Borders and Backgrounds

With WordPerfect, you easily can change the borders of **FIG-URE, TABLE, TEXT** and **USER-DEFINED BOX**es. These changes will affect all the boxes that follow in a document. However, these revised border or background definitions must appear before the first box you want to modify.

Type: ALT F9 (**GRAPHICS**)

Select: Option I (**FIGURE**)

Select: Option 4 (**OPTIONS**)

Response: You're presented with the **FIGURE BOX** options menu.

```
Options:    Figure

    1 - Border Style
            Left                        Single
            Right                       Single
            Top                         Single
            Bottom                      Single
    2 - Outside Border Space
            Left                        0.16"
            Right                       0.16"
            Top                         0.16"
            Bottom                      0.16"
    3 - Inside Border Space
            Left                        0"
            Right                       0"
            Top                         0"
            Bottom                      0"
    4 - First Level Numbering Method    Numbers
    5 - Second Level Numbering Method   Off
    6 - Caption Number Style            [BOLD]Figure 1[bold]
    7 - Position of Caption             Below box, Outside borders
    8 - Minimum Offset from Paragraph   0"
    9 - Gray Shading (% of black)       0%

Selection: 0
```

Select: Option 1 (**BORDER STYLE**)

Note the options available for each of the four sides of the **FIGURE BOX**:

Option 1 (**NONE**)
Option 2 (**SINGLE**)
Option 3 (**DOUBLE**)
Option 4 (**DASHED**)
Option 5 (**DOTTED**)
Option 6 (**THICK**)
Option 7 (**EXTRA THICK**)

For purposes of illustration, let's replace the **SINGLE** border default with an **EXTRA THICK** border.

Select: Option 7 (**EXTRA THICK**)

Response: This replaces the **SINGLE** left border default with the **EXTRA THICK** default. The cursor is advanced down to the right border setting. Again,

Select: Option 7 (**EXTRA THICK**)

Repeat this two more times, for the top and bottom borders, and preview your work.

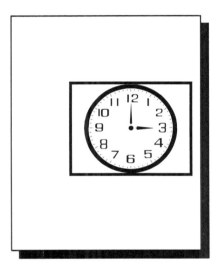

If you want the clock to "float" on the page, from the **BOR-DER STYLE** option,

Select: Option 1 (**NONE**) (for each of the borders.)

Adding Shaded Backgrounds to Figure Boxes

Return again to the **FIGURE BOX** options screen and replace the original thick and thin default borders.

Select: Option 9 (**GRAY SHADING (% OF BLACK)**)

Response: Note that the default is **0%,** which means that the graphic image appears against a white background.

Type: 20 (This changes the original **0%** default to **20%.**)

Preview or print.

Notice how the appearance of the graphic image has changed. The light gray background behind the graphic image helps distinguish it from the surrounding body copy.

Adding White Space around Boxes

Now you've seen how WordPerfect allows you to manipulate imported graphic images creatively—moving them, resizing them, distorting them and even in some cases reversing them. WordPerfect lets you orchestrate precisely the way the graphic images and their captions relate to surrounding headlines and body copy.

For example, you can adjust the amount of space between a

box and adjacent body copy. Adjusting the white space surrounding **FIGURE, TABLE, TEXT** and **USER-DEFINED BOX**es greatly influences the "color" of your document.

Type: ALT F9 (**GRAPHICS**)

Select: Option 1 (**FIGURE**)

Select: Option 4 (**OPTIONS**)

Select: Option 2 (**OUTSIDE BORDER SPACE**)

Response: The cursor advances to the 0.16 percent default for the left border.

Type: .5

Type: (RETURN)

Response: The cursor advances to the 0.16-inch default for the right border.

Type: .25

Type: (RETURN)

Response: The cursor advances to the 0.16-inch default for the top border.

Type: .5

Type: (RETURN)

Response: The cursor advances to the 0.16-inch default for the bottom border.

Type: 1

Type: (RETURN)

When you preview or print the page, the difference will be immediately apparent.

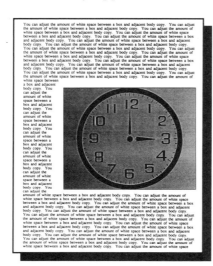 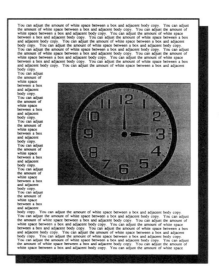

Adding White Space within Boxes

Likewise, you can adjust the internal space between a box and its contents.

Type: ALT F9 (**GRAPHICS**)

Select: Option 1 (**FIGURE**)

Select: Option 4 (**OPTIONS**)

Select: Option 3 (**INSIDE BORDER SPACE**)

Response: The cursor advances to the **0"** default for the inside left border.

As you did before, enter new figures and (**RETURN**) to change the defaults to the amount you want. That lets you add white space within boxes, again "opening up" the design of your document.

Compare this...

with this...

Captions

WordPerfect does most of the work involved in placing captions, which automatically extend the width of any **FIGURE, TABLE, TEXT** or **USER-DEFINED BOX** you create. If you change the dimensions of the box, the caption length automatically changes.

Compare this...

The time is 3:00 on the dot. Is it not?

with this...

The time is 3:00 on the dot. Is it not?

Placing Captions

WordPerfect lets you place captions either above or below **FIGURE, TABLE, TEXT** or **USER-DEFINED BOX**es.

Type: ALT F9 (**GRAPHICS**)

Select: Option 1 (**FIGURE**)

Select: Option 4 (**OPTIONS**)

Select: Option 7 (**POSITION OF CAPTION**)

Select: Option 1 (**BELOW BOX**)
or
Option 2 (**ABOVE BOX**)

Regardless of which option you choose, you then can decide whether you want to place the caption inside or next to the box.

Select: Option 1 (**OUTSIDE OF BORDER**)
or
Option 2 (**INSIDE OF BORDER**)

WordPerfect thus gives you four ways captions can relate to **FIGURE, TABLE, TEXT** or **USER-DEFINED BOX**es. By carefully using these alternatives, you can provide your document with a distinctive look.

The time is 3:00 on the dot. Is it not?

The time is 3:00 on the dot. Is it not?

Other Caption Options

WordPerfect makes it easy to define other caption attributes. For example, you can choose a specific caption numbering style, as well as define a typeface and type size to be used in all captions.

Type: ALT F9 (**GRAPHICS**)

Select: Option 1 (**FIGURE**)

Select: Option 4 (**OPTIONS**)

Select: Option 6 (**CAPTION NUMBER STYLE**)

Response: Replace with: (**BOLD**)Figure 1(**bold**)

At this point, you can eliminate the boldface type or, using WordPerfect's **FONT** command (CTRL F8) described in Chapter Six, define the specific type characteristics you want for the captions. You can, for example, choose a small italicized typeface and select either flush-left/ragged-right or justified lines of type.

You also can define the caption numbering scheme.

Type: ALT F9 (**GRAPHICS**)

Select: Option 1 (**FIGURE**)

Select: Option 4 (**OPTIONS**)

Select: Option 4 (**FIRST LEVEL NUMBERING METHOD**)

Response: Option 1 (**OFF**)
Option 2 (**NUMBERS**)
Option 3 (**LETTERS**)
Option 4 (**ROMAN NUMERALS**)

Select: Choose the option that best fits the graphic identity of your project.

Likewise, if you're using two-level caption numbering (each caption is numbered according to the chapter in which it's located) you can repeat the process and select a number scheme for second-level captions.

Type: ALT F9 (**GRAPHICS**)

Select: Option 1 (**FIGURE**)

Select: Option 4 (**OPTIONS**)

Select: Option 5 (**SECOND LEVEL NUMBERING METHOD**)

Response: Option 1 (**OFF**)
Option 2 (**NUMBERS**)
Option 3 (**LETTERS**)
Option 4 (**ROMAN NUMERALS**)

Select: Again, choose the option that best fits in with the graphic identity of your project.

Adjusting Minimum Paragraph Offset

WordPerfect lets you determine the minimum amount of white space that separates a box from an adjacent paragraph.

Type: ALT F9 (**GRAPHICS**)

Select: Option 1 (**FIGURE**)

Select: Option 4 (**OPTIONS**)

Select: Option 8 (**MINIMUM OFFSET FROM PARAGRAPH**)

Response: 0" (Default)

When placing a **PARAGRAPH BOX**, WordPerfect often reduces the white space between the paragraph and the box, in order to place both on the same page. This can lead to inconsistency, creating more space around some boxes than others.

However, you can specify a minimum value.

Type: .25

At least a quarter inch of white space will be maintained between the box and the top of the paragraph. If the paragraph is too long to allow for that on one page, the box will be shifted to the next page.

Overlapping Text and Graphics

There may be occasions when you would like words—particularly headlines—to be superimposed over graphic images. To place text over an existing **FIGURE BOX**,

Type: ALT F9 (**GRAPHICS**)

Select: Option 1 (**FIGURE**)

Select: Option 2 (**EDIT**)

Response: One number higher than the number of the last **FIGURE BOX** created.

Type: The number of the box over which you want to superimpose type.

Type: (RETURN)

Select: Option 7 (**WRAP TEXT AROUND BOX**)

Response: Yes (Default)

Type: N (**NO**)

Type: (RETURN)

This replaces the **YES** default. Type will be superimposed over the imported graphic.

Moving On

As the examples in this chapter indicate, desktop publishing with WordPerfect is made possible by careful definition and placement of **FIGURE, TABLE, TEXT** and **USER-DEFINED BOX**es. These boxes allow you to integrate your words with previously created charts, drawings, graphs, scanned photographs and text units, such as logos and mastheads.

In the next chapter, you'll learn some of the ways WordPerfect lets you control the placement and appearance of words. You'll find its typographic features to be as exciting as its ability to place and manipulate graphics.

6

Working with Type

What most distinguishes desktop-published materials from conventional typewritten documents? The answer is type—meaning the wealth of typefaces, type sizes and type styles that gives even the simplest document a professional look.

After all, which of the two resumes below would you prefer if you were an employer making a hiring decision or a job seeker applying for a job?

WordPerfect 5.0 makes it easy to incorporate a variety of typefaces, type sizes and type styles—bold, italics, etc.—into your projects, even while you're writing or editing them.

Type Influences Readership

"Font" is an all-encompassing term refering to a complete set of letters, numbers and symbols (asterisks, copyright symbols, etc.) which appear in a particular typeface, type size and type style.

By using WordPerfect's **FONT** command (CTRL F8), you can select or change the typeface, type size or type style used in your document while you're writing it. All words entered after the **FONT** command is exercised will appear in the newly selected type characteristics.

Or, you can use the **FONT** command while editing or formatting your document by highlighting the words or phrases you want to appear in a typeface, type size or type style different from that used for the unhighlighted text.

Typographical variations enhance the communicating power of your documents in several ways:

First, they help organize a hierarchy of information. Important words, such as headlines, can be made larger in order to attract more attention than supporting body copy.

Moreover, you can help readers quickly locate information by using subheads, which not only supplement headlines but highlight key sections throughout your document.

Finally, the use of different typefaces, type sizes and type styles provides visual contrast, keeping readers interested.

A Brief Review of Basic Typography

Five characteristics determine the way words and letters appear on the printed page: typeface, type size, attributes, alignment and spacing. Each characteristic is defined below.

Typeface

Each typeface has its own distinct appearance and personality, created by the shape of its letters. The thickness of the strokes of each letter and its decorative characteristics also affect the "look" of each typeface.

Each typeface speaks to readers in a different tone of voice. Some typefaces are formal, some are elegant, and others are authoritative. Some typefaces create an old-fashioned feeling, others a contemporary atmosphere. Some typefaces—often referred to as decorative or "display" faces—are best for head-lines. Other typefaces are better suited for body copy.

Park Avenue is an elegant typeface, ideally suited for formal invitations and menus for expensive restaurants.

You're Invited To The Grand Opening Of Our New Salon

Avant Garde has a clean, contemporary look.

Vision and Intuition, Architects and Planners, Inc.

Bookman has a decorative feel without being overdone.

Now You Can Enjoy Country Living In The City

A typeface visually colors a publication, influencing readership. Some typefaces are dense, with closely packed letters. Others spread the letters out, increasing readability. Notice the difference in line length between the three samples below, all set in the same type size:

The quick brown fox jumped.

The quick brown fox jumped.

The quick brown fox jumped.

Times Roman, a popular choice for body copy, allows many words to fit within a given space. Helvetica type spaces the letters farther apart.

Type Size

Type size is measured in points. There are 72 points to the inch. The body copy of this book appears in 10-point Palatino type. Surprisingly, the header at the top of each page also is set in 10-point type, even though the typeface and type style (Avant Garde bold) make it larger than 10-point Palatino Roman.

Chapter titles on the first page of each chapter are set in 40-point type. Subheads introducing the major subdivisions of each chapter are set in 11.5-point type. Secondary subheads are set in 10.5-point type while page numbers are set in 10-point type. Footnotes are set in 8-point type.

Attributes

Within each typeface are several variations, or attributes, in addition to regular (Roman) type. The most common include **boldface**, *italics* and <u>underlined</u>.

Alignment

Type can be placed flush-left, flush-right, centered or justified.

Most type is set flush-left. Flush type is easy to read, because the reader's eyes can locate the beginning of each line quickly.

Flush-left/ragged-right type is characterized by irregular line endings. Most lines break at the ends of words. Some lines break with hyphenation—words split by syllables. The irregular amounts of white space at the end of each line create documents with an "open" or "contemporary" feeling that invites the eye.

> The quick brown fox jumped over the lazy dog. The quick brown fox jumped over the lazy dog.

When type is justified, the first and last letters in each line are aligned with the first and last letters in the lines above and below it. WordPerfect subtly and automatically increases or decreases word spacing so that each line is of equal length.

> The quick brown fox jumped over the lazy dog. The quick brown fox jumped over the lazy dog.

Centered text is primarily used for headlines that contain no more than four lines of type. Centered text reduces readability, because readers have to make a conscious effort to find the beginning of each line.

The quick brown fox
jumped over the
lazy dog. The
quick brown fox
jumped over the
lazy dog.

Flush-right text also slows down reading and is best used for special applications. These include

- Relating subheads to body copy.

- Organizing lists so that related information in an adjacent column is as close as possible.

- Captions set to the left of a photograph or illustration.

- Short headlines.

The quick brown fox
jumped over the
lazy dog. The
quick brown fox
jumped over the
lazy dog.

Spacing

Letter, line, word and paragraph spacing have a great deal of influence on the appearance of the printed page.

As you'll explore in Chapter Seven, WordPerfect gives you the power to adjust letter spacing throughout your document or limit it to the spacing between selected pairs of letters, which can improve the readability and appearance of headlines.

Increasing word spacing can make a publication easier to read. Decreasing it allows you to include more words in your publication.

Likewise, you can visually "open up" a publication and make it more readable by increasing line spacing and adding extra space between paragraphs. Decreased line spacing creates stronger headlines, as does increasing the white space surrounding them.

Laser Printers

A serious discussion about typography is impossible without first taking a look at laser printers. Although millions of WordPerfect documents are printed every day on daisywheel or dot-matrix printers, serious desktop publishing requires access to a laser printer.

Because each laser printer is equipped with a set number of typefaces, the kind of printer you choose has a great deal of influence on the type options available to you.

The introduction of affordable laser printers made desktop publishing possible. These printers—which now cost between $2,000 and $6,000—offer nearly typeset quality at a fraction of the cost of phototypesetting machines or "first generation" laser printers (which used to cost nearly $100,000).

Laser printers fall into two primary families—PostScript and Hewlett-Packard laser printers. (Although Hewlett-Packard set the standard, dozens of printers made by other companies use those same standards. To easily identify them, let's refer to them as HP-compatible laser printers.)

First let's investigate the options available to owners of HP-compatible printers. Then we'll consider the options available to owners of PostScript printers, such as the Apple LaserWriter series. (If you already own a PostScript printer, skip to that section.)

With HP-compatible printers, multiple typefaces, type sizes and type styles are available in three ways: resident fonts, font cartridges and downloadable fonts.

Resident Fonts

HP-compatible printers contain resident fonts built into the electrical circuitry of the printers. The number of resident fonts depends upon the printer. Hewlett-Packard LaserJet Series II, for example, includes Courier—a typeface resembling a standard typewriter—Courier Bold, and a Line Printer font with letters spaced extremely close together. These fonts are available in 12- and 8.5-point type.

Resident fonts can be placed on the page in either portrait or landscape orientation. Portrait orientation refers to lines of type that extend across the short dimension of an 8 1/2- by 11-inch sheet of paper, the format of a standard letter. With landscape orientation, type extends across the long, or 11-inch, dimension of paper.

The limitations of Hewlett-Packard LaserJet II's resident fonts are obvious. Printed pages resemble typewritten pages. Serious desktop publishing requires a wider variety of typefaces, type sizes and type styles, available as extra cost options.

Font Cartridges

The easiest and least expensive way to add typefaces to your HP-compatible printer is to plug in one or more font cartridges, each of which includes a limited selection of typeface, type size and type style choices.

The Microsoft "Z" cartridge, for example, offers four type size variations of two of the most widely used typefaces available—Helvetica and Times Roman. Two type sizes are available in three styles: medium, bold and italics. The Microsoft "Z" cartridge includes

14 point Helv bold

12 point Helv bold
12 point Helv medium
12 point Helv italic

10 point Helv bold
10 point Helv medium
10 point Helv italic

8 point Helv medium

14 point TmsRmn bold

12 point TmsRmn bold
12 point TmsRmn medium
12 point TmsRmn italic

10 point TmsRmn bold
10 point TmsRmn medium
10 point TmsRmn italic

8 point TmsRmn medium

Note that "Helv" and "TmsRmn" are variations on the original Helvetica and Times Roman typefaces, licensed from the International Typographic Corporation (ITC). If you were to make a letter-by-letter comparison of the samples above with the actual ITC fonts, you would probably notice slight variations in the design of individual letters.

Installing HP Font Cartridges

WordPerfect makes it easy to select typeface, type size and type style alternatives with font cartridges. As you read about font cartridge installation below, remember that the process can be speeded up by creating macros or stylesheets.

To install a new font cartridge in your laser printer,

Type: SHFT F7 (**PRINT**)

Select: Option S (**SELECT PRINTER**)

Response: You're presented with the name of the currently chosen printer. (Several names can be listed. An asterisk appears next to the one currently selected.)

Select: Option 3 (**EDIT**)

Select: Option 5 (**CARTRIDGES AND FONTS**)

Select: Option 1 (**SELECT FONTS**)

Response: Your screen now is filled with a list of all available fonts.

Use the up or down cursor control keys to scroll through the list until the font cartridge you want to install is highlighted. Then press (**RETURN**). An asterisk will appear next to the cartridge you've selected, indicating that it's available for use.

If you're installing more than one font cartridge, follow the same procedure to select the second.

To exit the font selection process, press WordPerfect's **EXIT** command (F7) twice. A prompt at the bottom of the screen will indicate that screen fonts are being updated.

When files have been updated, you'll be returned to the **SELECT PRINTER: EDIT** screen. To return to your document,

Type: (RETURN) (RETURN) (RETURN)

You're now ready to begin work.

Downloadable Fonts

Downloadable, or *soft*, fonts offer a wider, richer selection of typefaces and type sizes. However, they must be loaded into your printer's memory each time you turn on the printer. WordPerfect makes it easy to use downloadable fonts by automatically loading them at the start of your working session and deleting them after your document is printed.

Because they take up a great deal of printer memory, Word-Perfect's "font-swapping" feature conserves precious printer memory, at the same time giving you a wider choice of fonts.

Downloadable fonts are available from Hewlett-Packard, Adobe, Bitstream and others. Hewlett-Packard downloadable fonts are available in sizes up to 34 points, so you can include larger headlines in your documents. Downloadable fonts from other firms allow you to create even larger headlines.

Downloadable fonts also let you take advantage of typographic refinements described in the next chapter, such as kerning (the ability to adjust the spacing between individual pairs of letters). In addition, by combining downloadable fonts with software programs available from firms such as Softcraft, you can create reversed or shaded type effects that can't be achieved with resident fonts or font cartridges.

Reversed type appears as white type against a black background.

Shaded type appears in various shades of gray, instead of 100 percent black.

The number of downloadable fonts available to you is determined by your printer's memory. Additional printer memory allows you to include a wider variety of typefaces in your documents (as well as larger graphic images).

Installing Downloadable Fonts

To add downloadable fonts to your typeface alternatives,

Select: SHFT F7 (**PRINT**)

Select: Option S (**SELECT PRINTER**)

Select: Option 3 (**EDIT**)

Select: Option 7 (**PATH FOR DOWNLOADABLE FONTS AND PRINTER COMMAND FILES**)

Type: Specify the name of the subdirectory where you've stored the font files, if you haven't included them with your Word-Perfect files.

Select: Option 5 (**CARTRIDGES AND FONTS**)

Type: Scroll down to **SOFT FONTS**. (This only applies to LaserJet.)

Select: Option 1 (**SELECT FONTS**)

You'll then be presented with an alphabetical list of all font files in the selected subdirectory, sorted by type specifications (e.g., bold or italics).

Scroll down until you reach the first typeface, size and style alternative you want to include in your document.

If you want the font always to be available when printing begins,

Type: SHFT 8 (**ASTERISK**)

Or, if you want to conserve printer memory, which will let you include larger graphic images on each page, and only download the font when it's needed,

Select: + (**PLUS SIGN**)

You now have access to the fonts already downloaded to your printer or stored on your hard disk. Before you put these fonts to work, let's consider the other major printer family, based on the PostScript Page Description Language.

PostScript Printers

PostScript-based printers, such as the Apple LaserWriter Plus and LaserWriter II NT, offer a richer choice of type characteristics than do HP-compatible printers. Without adding downloadable fonts, you immediately have access to a wide selection of built-in typefaces, each of which can be reproduced in any point size or style from small to large, from regular to bold—to even boldface italics.

PostScript's flexibility stems from its ability to define the shape—or outline—of letters, numbers and drawings as a series of coordinates, which are similar to latitude and longitude markings on a map. The shape of each letter, number and part of a drawing is defined by identifying the starting and ending points of the numerous lines that comprise its outline. After the letters and numbers have been outlined, the space between the outlines is shaded (filled in).

PostScript printers have virtually unlimited type size variations. Because you're not limited to the sizes built into font cartridges or downloadable files, you can specify each typeface in any size from one point to letters that are large enough to fill an entire page! You can even include half-point sizes (e.g., 8.5-point type).

In addition, you can achieve creative effects by rotating type or creating mirror graphic images.

For example, you can rotate type 90 degrees to create a vertical newsletter masthead. You also can place photo credits in a vertical position next to the photographs, where they won't interfere with captions or body copy.

Routine illustrations or scanned photographs can be enhanced creatively by using mirror images.

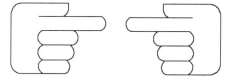

PostScript laser printers also offer typographic refinements, such as kerning (the ability to adjust the spacing between individual pairs of letters) and tracking (the ability to adjust letter spacing throughout a document) without purchasing additional downloadable fonts or font-manipulation programs.

You also can create reversed headlines—white type against a black background—without additional purchases. (With HP-compatible printers, additional software programs are required to achieve these effects.)

The original Apple LaserWriter Plus has been augmented by PostScript printers from numerous other vendors, such as AST, QMS and a new generation of Apple laser printers, such as the Apple LaserWriter II NT.

One choice, the Apple LaserWriter II NT, easily can be connected to your computer through the standard printer RS-232 connection. Like the original LaserWriter Plus, it features several built-in typefaces. In addition to the basic "typewriter-style" Courier type, its type choices include

Palatino	ITC Avant Garde Gothic Book
Palatino Bold	*ITC Avant Garde Gothic Book Oblique*
Palatino Bold Italic	**ITC Avant Garde Gothic Demi**
Palatino Italic	***ITC Avant Garde Gothic Demi Oblique***
Times Roman	**ITC Bookman Demi**
Times Roman Bold	***ITC Bookman Demi Italic***
Times Roman Bold Italic	ITC Bookman Light
Times Roman Italic	*ITC Bookman Light Italic*
Helvetica	*ITC Zapf Chancery Medium Italic*
Helvetica Bold	*ITC Zapf Dingbats*
Helvetica Bold Oblique	Symbol
Helvetica Narrow	New Century Schoolbook
Helvetica Narrow Bold	**New Century Schoolbook Bold**
Helvetica Narrow Bold Oblique	***New Century Schoolbook Bold Italic***
Helvetica Narrow Oblique	*New Century Schoolbook Italic*

Boldface, italic and boldface/italic variations of each typeface also are available.

The Apple LaserWriter II SC, primarily designed for use with the Macintosh, only includes four built-in typefaces (Courier, Symbol, Helvetica and Times). The LaserWriter II NTX offers the same typeface alternatives as the LaserWriter II NT, but operates faster and easily can be hooked up to more than one computer.

PostScript Font Options

Although PostScript font cartridges aren't available, a full range of downloadable fonts can be added to a PostScript printer. They're available from a variety of independent vendors, such as Adobe and Bitstream.

The process of adding downloadable fonts to PostScript printers is similar to that of adding downloadable fonts to HP-compatible printers.

Type: F7 (**PRINT**)

Select: Option S (**SELECT PRINTER**)

Select: Option 3 (**EDIT**)

Select: Option 5 (**CARTRIDGES AND FONTS**)

Response: Downloadable Fonts

Type: Option 1 (**SELECT**)

You're presented with a list of all available downloadable fonts installed in your hard disk. Scroll through the list using your up/down cursor control keys. When you highlight a font, you want to download automatically when you begin working,

Type: *

If you want a font only to be downloaded when it's needed to print a particular part of your document,

Type: +

> After you've finished selecting the fonts you want to use in your project,

Type: F7 (**EXIT**)

Type: F7 (**EXIT**)

Type: (RETURN) (RETURN) (RETURN)

QMS JetScript

Owners of Hewlett-Packard Series II printers can upgrade to PostScript by adding the QMS JetScript, a hardware and software package that adds PostScript compatibility.

The QMS JetScript consists of software and two plug-in circuit boards (one of which is added to an expansion slot in your computer, the other to your printer). The QMS JetScript offers an easy migration path to LaserJet printer owners who want the flexibility and additional resident fonts of a PostScript printer without having to replace their original printer.

The QMS JetScript is easily installed and doesn't affect the normal operation of the printer. Nor does it alter the LaserJet Series II's warranty.

Working with Fonts

The first step in creating a desktop-published document is to choose a particular typeface, type size or type style that will be used for the majority of your documents. These specifications will be referred to as the **INITIAL FONT**, which will be the default font chosen, unless you select a different font.

To choose an **INITIAL FONT**,

Type: SHFT F7 (**PRINT**)

Select: Option S (**SELECT PRINTER**)

Response: You're presented with a list of printers you've previously chosen. The currently active printer will be highlighted and appear with an asterisk. If this is the printer you'll be working with,

Type: (RETURN)

If you're working with more than two printers and wish to switch to a different printer, scroll down until the printer you want is highlighted, then

Type: (RETURN)

Select: Option 3 (**EDIT**)

Select: Option 6 (**INITIAL FONT**)

Response: Your printer's particular default resident font will be replaced by an alphabetical list of all typefaces and type styles available as resident fonts, downloadable fonts and, in the case of HP-compatible printers, font cartridges.

Type: Use your up/down cursor control keys to scroll down until you reach the particular font you want to choose as a default font.

Type: (RETURN)

Response: If your printer is HP-compatible, your options include the specific type sizes available.

If, however, you're using a PostScript printer, you must select the default type size. Note that **10** appears at the lower left of your screen. If you want to use 10-point type as the default,

Type: (RETURN)

If, however, you want your **INITIAL FONT** to be larger or smaller, enter the particular type size you want. For example,

Type: 12

Type: (RETURN)

To return to your editing screen,

Type: (RETURN) (RETURN) (RETURN)

Choosing a Base Font

Often, you'll want to choose a different typeface, type size and type style to use for a particular project. WordPerfect offers a **BASE FONT** feature that makes it easy to choose a particular set of type specifications for a project, regardless of the type of printer you use.

To choose a **BASE FONT**,

Type: CTRL F8 (**FONT**)

Select: Option 4 (**BASE FONT**)

The screen then displays an alphabetical list of all available type alternatives, which includes your currently selected printer's resident fonts and any font cartridges or download-able fonts you've installed.

```
Base Font

► Courier
  Courier Bold
  Courier Bold Oblique
  Courier Oblique
  Helvetica
  Helvetica Bold
  Helvetica Bold Oblique
  Helvetica Narrow
  Helvetica Narrow Bold
  Helvetica Narrow Bold Oblique
  Helvetica Narrow Oblique
  Helvetica Oblique
  ITC Avant Garde Gothic Book
  ITC Avant Garde Gothic Book Oblique
  ITC Avant Garde Gothic Demi
  ITC Avant Garde Gothic Demi Oblique
  ITC Bookman Demi
  ITC Bookman Demi Italic
  ITC Bookman Light
  ITC Bookman Light Italic
  ITC Zapf Chancery Medium Italic

1 Select; N Name search: 1
```

Scroll down until your typeface choice is highlighted. If you're using an HP-compatible printer, note that a type size accompanies each typeface and type style alternative. When you come to the font alternative you want to use throughout your document,

Select: Option 1 (**SELECT**)
or (RETURN)

If you're using an·HP-compatible printer, your type size is chosen automatically when you choose the typeface and style.

If, however, you're using a PostScript printer, you'll be prompted to choose a type size.

Type: 12 (or the size you want.)

Type: (RETURN)

Response: This replaces the 10-point default with the type size you want for your **BASE FONT**.

You then will be returned to your document automatically. All the text that follows will appear in the type options you just chose, as will everything you type from that point forward. These type specifications will continue to be used until you either select a new **BASE FONT** or a new type size or style.

Screen Display

Note that unless you've installed the Hercules RamFont video card described in Appendix A, the size and appearance of the type on your screen will remain the same regardless of what you've chosen. This important point reflects one area in which WordPerfect differs from dedicated page layout programs.

To double-check your **BASE FONT**, use WordPerfect's **REVEAL CODES** command (ALT F3) or **VIEW DOCUMENT** (SHFT F7, 6).

Choosing Larger or Smaller Type

Regardless of the type of printer you're using, you easily can choose larger or smaller type sizes while you're writing or editing your document. This makes it easy to create a very visible hierarchy of information, ranging from large headlines and smaller subheads to even smaller body copy and captions.

WordPerfect offers a shortcut that automatically changes type size to the next available alternative, larger or smaller. You can use this valuable time-saving feature while entering new text or by blocking previously entered text.

To change the type size of new text,

Type: CTRL F8 (**FONT**)

Select: Option 1 (**SIZE**)

Response: You're presented with the following size options:

Option 1 **SUPRSCPT** (Superscript—letters raised above their original baseline, or regular vertical position)
Option 2 **SUBSCPT** (Subscript—letters placed below their original baseline, or normal vertical position)
Option 3 **FINE**
Option 4 **SMALL**
Option 5 **LARGE**
Option 6 **VRY LARGE** (Very Large)
Option 7 **EXT LARGE** (Extra Large)

Type: The number, or alphabet shortcut, that describes the type size you want.

For purposes of illustration,

Select: Option 5 (**LARGE**)

If you're using a color monitor, the words you've highlighted will appear on your screen in a different color. When printed, the words will be larger than the **BASE FONT**.

This base font is Times Roman 10 point.

Now you have selected LARGE type.

Text entered from this point on will be in the newly selected type size.

Remember that the type sizes chosen for **FINE, SMALL, LARGE**, etc., are determined both by the type sizes available on your computer, as well as the size of the **BASE FONT** you've chosen. As the illustrations below show, type sizes which relate to a PostScript, Times Roman, 10-point **BASE FONT** are different from those that relate to a Times Roman, 12-point **BASE FONT**.

10-point BASE FONT-FINE

10-point BASE FONT-LARGE

12-point BASE FONT-FINE

12-point BASE FONT-LARGE

Use **VIEW DOCUMENT** (SHFT F7, 6) or **PRINT** (SHFT F7, 2) to preview your work.

Returning to Base Font

To return to the **BASE FONT** chosen for this particular project,

Type: CTRL F8 (**FONT**)

Select: Option 4 (**BASE FONT**)

Text entered after this point will be set in the typeface and type size you've defined as your **BASE FONT**.

Choosing a Particular Type Size

Although WordPerfect's **BASE FONT** feature is used primarily to establish a default for the body copy in your document, you also can use it to choose a particular type size for a special purpose—such as a headline. Users of PostScript printers probably will make frequent use of this feature.

Let's assume you want to create a headline set in 48-point Helvetica type.

Type: CTRL F8 (**FONT**)

Select: Option 4 (**BASE FONT**)

Response: A list of all available resident and downloadable fonts will appear.

Type: Use your cursor control key to select the particular typeface you want for your headline—in this case, Helvetica.

Response: Type size: 10 (or the previously chosen **BASE FONT** type size.)

Type: 48

Type: (RETURN)

Response: You'll be returned to the editing screen.

TIP: After you've modified the **BASE FONT** to select a specific headline typeface and type size, you must repeat the process to reselect the **BASE FONT** you were using for the majority of the text in your document.

187

Changing Type Size in Previously Entered Text

It's even easier to change the type size of previously entered text. First, select—or highlight—the text you want modified.

Type: ALT F4 (**BLOCK**)

Type: (CTRL) Right Cursor Control Key

This highlights the letter to the right of the cursor. Use (**CTRL**) plus the right cursor control key to highlight one word at a time. Use (**HOME**) (**HOME**) and the right cursor control key to highlight the remainder of the line. Use the down cursor control key to advance blocking through the next line.

After you've highlighted all the words in the passage,

Type: CTRL F8 (**FONT**)

Response: You're presented with two alternatives:

Option 1 (**SIZE**)
Option 2 (**APPEARANCE**)

Select: Option 1 (**SIZE**)

Response: You're again presented with the following size alternatives:

Option 1 **SUPRSCPT** (Superscript—letters raised above their
     original baseline, or normal vertical position)
Option 2 **SUBSCPT** (Subscript—letters placed below their
     original baseline, or normal vertical position)
Option 3 **FINE**
Option 4 **SMALL**
Option 5 **LARGE**
Option 6 **VRY LARGE** (Very Large)
Option 7 **EXT LARGE** (Extra Large)

Select: The size alternative you want.

Response: You immediately will return to your normal editing screen.

Changing Type Styles in New Text

In a similar way, you can change the appearance of previously entered text or new text as you enter it. You can emphasize certain words by underlining them or setting them in boldface or italic type.

To change the appearance of new text,

Type: CTRL F8 (**FONT**)

Select: Option 2 (**APPEARANCE**)

Response: The following choices appear on your screen:

Option 1 (**BOLD**)
Option 2 (**UNDRLN**) (underline)
Option 3 (**DBL UND**) (double underline)
Option 4 (**ITALC**) (italics)
Option 5 (**OUTLN**) (outline)
Option 6 (**SHADW**) (shadow)
Option 7 (**SM CAP**) (small upper-case)
Option 8 (**REDLN**) (redline. This highlights text or places dark text against a white background. It's a technique used to indicate that text has been added or modified useful when two or more individuals are editing a document.)
Option 9 (**STKOUT**) (strikeout—a favorite used to indicate changes in legal documents.)

For purposes of illustration,

Select: Option 1 (**BOLD**)

Response: You'll be returned to your normal editing screen.

TIP: If you've added the Hercules RamFont card, any words you enter from this point on will be visibly darkened on the screen.

As a further illustration, if you have the RamFont card and a PostScript printer,

Type: CTRL 8 (**FONT**)

Select: Option 2 (**APPEARANCE**)

Select: Option 4 (**ITALICS**)

Response: You'll be returned to the editing screen and new text will appear in bold italics.

Returning to Normal Type Style with New Text

To return to normal (or Roman) text after changing to bold, italics or any other option,

Type: CTRL F8 (**FONT**)

Select: Option 3 (**NORMAL**)

Response: You'll be returned to your document, and newly entered text will appear in Roman.

TIP: After completing the above exercise, use WordPerfect's **VIEW DOCUMENT** (SHFT F7, 6) to observe how the type styles have alternated between bold, italics and Roman. **PRINT** (SHFT F7, 2) to see how these screen images translate to the printed page.

Changing Type Styles of Previously Entered Text

While editing your document, you can change the appearance of previously entered text.

Type: ALT F4 (**BLOCK**)

Type: As before, use your cursor control keys to highlight text to be changed.

Type: CTRL F8 (**FONT**)

Select: Option 2 (**APPEARANCE**)

Response: Again, the following choices appear on your screen:
Option 1 (**BOLD**)
Option 2 (**UNDRLN**) (underline)
Option 3 (**DBL UND**) (double underline)
Option 4 (**ITALC**) (italics)
Option 5 (**OUTLN**) (outline)
Option 6 (**SHADW**) (shadow)
Option 7 (**SM CAP**) (small upper-case)
Option 8 (**REDLN**) (redline)
Option 9 (**STKOUT**) (strikeout)

TIP: Remember that you can still use the regular WordPerfect **BOLD** (F6) and **UNDERLINE** (F8) commands which haven't changed from earlier versions. They can be used when entering new text or applied to highlighted text.

After you've changed the type style of previously entered text by highlighting it, you automatically are returned to your previously selected **BASE FONT**. You do not need to select **NORMAL** (Option 3).

Color Monitors

One of the advantages of using WordPerfect 5.0 with a color monitor is that you can use different combinations of background and foreground colors to indicate which type size or style is currently being used.

To choose colors,

Type: SHFT F1 (**SETUP**)

Select: Option 3 (**DISPLAY**)

Select: Option 2 (**COLORS/FONTS/ATTRIBUTES**)

Select: Option 1 (**SCREEN COLORS**)

Response: Depending upon which color monitor you use, you'll be able to assign different foreground and background colors

191

for the various type sizes and styles you'll be using in your document.

Use your up/down and left/right cursor control keys to locate the size and style attributes you want to highlight. Move the cursor to **FOREGROUND** or **BACKGROUND** columns and type the letter corresponding to the colors you want. Notice that the "sample" column immediately shows you how the particular mixture of your foreground and background colors will appear on your screen.

When you're finished,

Type: F7 (**EXIT**)

Type: (RETURN) (RETURN) (RETURN)

This returns you to your editing screen.

TIP: As with previous versions, WordPerfect 5.0 lets you write and edit two documents simultaneously, changing between them by using the **SWITCH** command (SHFT F3). You can choose the same background colors for both Document A and Document B or different background colors for each document (which lets you know at a glance which document you're working on).

Moving On

In this chapter, you reviewed the basic WordPerfect commands for creating attractive, easy-to-read documents based on the use of multiple typefaces, sizes and styles.

In the next chapter, "Typographic Refinements," you'll delve deeper into WordPerfect's ability to manipulate the appearance and placement of text. You'll find that WordPerfect 5.0 rivals dedicated desktop publishing programs—and even expensive phototypesetting systems—in its ability to let you precisely adjust letter, word, line and paragraph spacing as well as create special effects like reversed and shaded type.

With typographic refinements, you can create attention-getting publications that look as if they were professionally typeset.

7

Typographic Refinements

Creating attractive, readable documents involves many design considerations. Among the most important decisions is where to place type on a page, which also involves defining the spacing between letters, words, lines and paragraphs. Word-Perfect makes it easy to set and adjust spacing, as well as hyphenation.

As with other type-related features, your printer and the type of fonts you use determine the degree to which you can use WordPerfect's spacing and hyphenation features.

For example, users of HP-compatible printers must have downloadable fonts to take full advantage of WordPerfect's ability to manipulate letter, word and line spacing precisely. However, these refinements are immediately available to PostScript printer users, because WordPerfect can adjust the spacing of PostScript's resident fonts.

Finally, in this chapter, you'll learn the steps necessary to create and refine a high-impact reversed headline with a PostScript printer. Nothing attracts attention like white words appearing against a black background! You'll also look at WordPerfect's ability to create type in shades of gray.

(Owners of HP-compatible printers who want the same features should read Appendix C, an introduction to the various SoftCraft programs that give those printers capabilities similar to those of a PostScript printer.)

Advanced Typographic Terms

Kerning

Kerning refers to adjusting the space between selected pairs, or groups, of letters. Decreased letter spacing creates words out of otherwise isolated letters. Increased letter spacing emphasizes otherwise "lost" letters—such as a lower-case "i" dwarfed between an "l" and a "t."

Tracking

Tracking refers to increasing or decreasing letter spacing throughout a document, as opposed to kerning, which applies only to the spacing of certain letters.

Leading

Leading is the term for line spacing. The appearance of headlines often can be improved by reducing line spacing, which creates a tighter grouping of words. Line spacing also can be increased. For example, if you want to give a headline more impact, you can increase line spacing and add horizontal lines beneath the headline.

Widows and Orphans

A widow is a single word or syllable isolated by itself at the end of a paragraph, column or page. An orphan occurs when the last line of a paragraph appears by itself at the top of a column or the beginning of the following page. Widows and orphans are unsightly, stranded words that occupy an entire line, distracting readers and playing havoc with an otherwise tight page layout.

WordPerfect has a special feature that protects copy from widows and orphans, thus improving the appearance of your document.

Kerning with WordPerfect

Kerning becomes increasingly important as type size increases. Normal letter spacing for some combinations of letters (e.g., an upper-case "W" next to a lower-case "a") becomes noticeably exaggerated when set in large type.

WordPerfect's kerning capability lets you reduce letter spacing to compensate for that. The result is a more pleasing headline for your brochure or newsletter. Compare these two examples.

Wave
Wave

Based on the resident and downloadable fonts you use, WordPerfect offers both automatic and selective kerning.

The example below illustrates how kerning can improve the appearance of a headline, based on a resident font in a PostScript printer. To begin, turn off justification:

Type: SHFT F8 (**FORMAT**)

Select: Option 1 (**LINE**)

Select: Option 3 (**JUSTIFICATION**)

Response: If the cursor is blinking under **No**, press (**RETURN**). If the cursor is blinking under **Yes**,

Type: N

Type: (RETURN) (RETURN)

You're returned to your editing screen and are ready to get down to business.

Type:	CTRL F8 (**FONT**)
Select:	Option 4 (**BASE FONT**)
Response:	You're presented with an alphabetical list of all available resident and downloaded fonts.
Select:	Helvetica
Response:	Point size: 10
Type:	40
Type:	World Kerning Conference
Response:	Preview your work using WordPerfect's **VIEW DOCUMENT** command (SHFT F7, 6). Select **100%** or **200%** magnification to get a closer look at the letter spacing.

Note the gaps between the upper-case **W** and the lower-case **o**, and the upper-case **K** and the lower-case **e,** as well the large space separating the upper-case **C** and the lower-case **o**.

To have a permanent record of a headline that hasn't been kerned, **PRINT** the page (SHFT F7, 2).

World Kerning Conference

Automatic Kerning

To apply automatic kerning, place the cursor in front of the **W** and

Type: SHFT F8 (**FORMAT**)

Select: Option 4 (**OTHER**)

Select: Option 6 (**PRINTER FUNCTIONS**)

Select: Option 1 (**KERNING**)

Response: The cursor will blink under the word **No**.

Type: Y

Type: (RETURN) (RETURN) (RETURN)

Use WordPerfect's **VIEW DOCUMENT** command (SHFT F7, 6) at **100%** or **200%** to preview your work, or **PRINT** the page (SHFT F7, 2). Compare it with the page you printed before you selected the **KERNING** feature. Notice the improvement in letter spacing. Certain pairs of letters have been pulled closer together.

Selective Kerning

You also can adjust letter spacing on a more selective basis. Instead of using WordPerfect's automatic kerning feature, you can choose to adjust individual letter pairs precisely. To illustrate, let's reduce the spacing between the **W** and the **o** in **World**.

Type: Place the cursor in front of the **W**.

Type: SHFT F8 (**FORMAT**)

Select: Option 4 (**OTHER**)

Select: Option 6 (**PRINTER FUNCTIONS**)

Select: Option 3 (**WORD SPACING**)

Response: Option 1 (**NORMAL**) This setting looks best, according to the printer manufacturer.

Option 2 (**OPTIMAL**) This setting looks best, according to the WordPerfect Corp. (often the same setting as Option 1).

Option 3 (**PERCENT OF OPTIMAL**) Numbers less than 100 percent reduce space from the WordPerfect **OPTIMAL**; numbers greater than 100 percent increase space from **OPTIMAL**.

Option 4 (**SET PITCH**) You can specify the exact number of characters per inch.

Type: (RETURN)

This accepts the Option 2 (**OPTIMAL**) default and advances you to the **LETTER SPACING** menu, which lists four options:

Option 1 (**NORMAL**)

Option 2 (**OPTIMAL**) This adjusts letter spacing on the basis of type size.

Option 3 (**PERCENT OF OPTIMAL**)

Option 4 (**SET PITCH**)

You now can adjust letter spacing from this point in your document forward. The setting you choose will remain in effect until you advance the cursor past the **o** and return letter spacing to normal.

Select: Option 3 (**PERCENT OF OPTIMAL**)

Response: 100

Type: 85

Type: (RETURN) (RETURN) (RETURN)

This returns you to your editing screen. **VIEW DOCUMENT** (SHFT F7, 6) or **PRINT** (SHFT F7, 2). Notice the difference in the letter spacing.

You can expand letter spacing in a similar way. Take for example the way a lower-case "i" is obscured when placed between an "l" and a "t." You easily can add a little air around the "i" by slightly increasing letter spacing. Again, it's a three-step process:

1. Start by positioning the cursor before the letter pairs you want to expand.

2. Using the **LETTER SPACING** feature found in the **PRINTER FUNCTION** menu, add space (e.g., replace the **100%** default with **110%** of optimal).

3. Position the cursor after the letter pairs you want to expand and return letter spacing to normal.

lite
lite

Returning to Normal Letter Spacing

To return to regular letter spacing, advance the cursor until it's between the **o** and the **r**. Then,

Type:	SHFT F8 (**FORMAT**)
Select:	Option 4 (**OTHER**)
Select:	Option 6 (**PRINTER FUNCTIONS**)
Select:	Option 3 (**WORD SPACING**)
Select:	Option 2 (**OPTIMAL**)
Response:	This advances you to the **LETTER SPACING** menu.
Select:	Option 2 (**OPTIMAL**)
Type:	(RETURN) (RETURN) (RETURN)

199

Type: F7 (**EXIT**)

VIEW DOCUMENT (SHFT F7, 6) or **PRINT** (SHFT F7, 2). The difference will be apparent immediately. The letters which follow the **o** are now spaced farther apart.

Creative Applications

You can use WordPerfect's **SET PITCH** command (SHFT F8, 4, 6, 3) to create exaggerated letter spacing for special effects, such as departmental headers in a newsletter (e.g., "Upcoming Events"). The **SET PITCH** command allows you to specify the number of characters per inch, automatically choosing the correct spacing.

To illustrate this important feature, let's assume you have a PostScript printer and want to create centered departmental headings using widely spaced, upper-case, 14-point, Times Roman type.

Type: CTRL F8 (**FONT**)

Select: Option 4 (**BASE FONT**)

Response: You're presented with a list of available resident and down-loaded fonts.

Type: Scroll down until **TIMES ROMAN** appears.

Type: (RETURN)

Response: Type size: 10 (or last chosen type size.)

Type: 14

Type: (CAPS LOCK) (**CAPITAL LOCK**)

Type: Upcoming Events

Type: (RETURN)

The above gives you a frame of reference for the effects of WordPerfect's powerful **SET PITCH** command. To continue,

Type: SHFT F8 (**FORMAT**)

Select: Option 4 (**OTHER**)

Select: Option 6 (**PRINTER FUNCTIONS**)

Select: Option 3 (**WORD SPACING**)

Response: The various word-spacing options appear.

Type: (RETURN) (to accept Option 2 (**OPTIMAL**).)

Response: The various letter-spacing options appear.

Select: Option 4 (**SET PITCH**)

Response: 9.3 (The pitch that corresponds to the default's **OPTIMAL** setting.)

Type: 6

Type: (RETURN)

Type: Upcoming Events

Type: (RETURN)

This indicates that you want six characters per inch. You then are returned to the editing screen. By using the **VIEW DOCUMENT** command (SHFT F7, 6) or **PRINT** (SHFT F7, 2), you will be able to see the difference immediately.

UPCOMING EVENTS
UPCOMING EVENTS

Adjusting Word Spacing

WordPerfect lets you adjust word spacing to fine-tune the appearance of your document, as well as adjust the word density. Adjusting space between words also lets you "lighten" or "darken" a publication.

To modify word spacing, advance your cursor to the beginning of your document. The quickest way to do that is to use WordPerfect's **HOME** command ([HOME] [HOME] Up Cursor Control Key). Then,

Type: SHFT F8 (**FORMAT**)

Select: Option 4 (**OTHER**)

Select: Option 6 (**PRINTER FUNCTIONS**)

Select: Option 3 (**WORD SPACING**)

Response: You're presented with the following choices:

Option 1 (**NORMAL**)
Option 2 (**OPTIMAL**)
Option 3 (**PERCENT OF OPTIMAL**)
Option 4 (**SET PITCH**)

Select: Option 3 (**PERCENT OF OPTIMAL**)

If you want word spacing to be reduced and density increased, type in a figure less than 100. If you want to spread out word spacing, enter a figure greater than 100. This command is useful when you're working with narrow columns and too many words are being hyphenated.

TIP: Just as **SET PITCH** was used as a creative tool in the letter-spacing example above, you can use **SET PITCH** to force unnaturally wide or narrow spaces between words to create special, exaggerated effects.

Adjusting Line Spacing

With WordPerfect 5.0, you also can modify leading (line spacing). Again, this refinement becomes extremely important as type size increases. The appearance of headlines set on several lines, for example, is often greatly improved by reduced line spacing. Tighter spacing makes a headline look more like a unit, rather than a series of unrelated lines of type.

Start by creating a centered multi-line headline (be sure to turn justification **OFF**):

Type: CTRL F8 (**FONT**)

Select: Option 4 (**BASE FONT**)

Response: A list of all available resident and downloadable fonts.

Scroll down until you reach **HELVETICA BOLD**.

Type: (RETURN)

Response: Point size: 10 (or last chosen type size.)

Type: 24

Type: (RETURN)

Type: AMAZING DISCOVERY No Need to Change Vacuum Cleaner Bags

Type: (RETURN) (after **DISCOVERY**)

Type: (RETURN) (after **Change**)

Return to the beginning of the headline.

Type: ALT F4 (**BLOCK**)

Move the cursor to the end of the headline.

Type: SHFT F6 (**CENTER**)

Response: (Cntr)? (Y/N) No

Type: Y

Response: This creates a centered three-line headline.

To reduce line height, place your cursor at the beginning of the headline,

Type: SHFT F8 (**FORMAT**)

Select: Option 1 (**LINE**)

Response: You're presented with the **FORMAT: LINE** menu, which lists numerous options.

Select: Option 4 (**LINE HEIGHT**)

Response: You're presented with two alternatives:

Option 1 (**AUTO**)
Option 2 (**FIXED**)

Select: Option 2 (**FIXED**)

Response: 0.35"

Type: .30

Type: (RETURN) (RETURN)

When you **VIEW DOCUMENT** (SHFT F7, 6) or **PRINT** (SHFT F7, 2), the change will be readily apparent.

AMAZING DISCOVERY
No Need to Change
Vacuum Cleaner Bags.

There may be occasions when you want to increase line height—for instance, if you want to emphasize a headline by adding horizontal rules under the words. In that case, you might want to choose line height of three-quarters of an inch.

AMAZING DISCOVERY

No Need to Change

Vacuum Cleaner Bags.

Adjusting White Space at the Beginning of Lines

One of the ways you can control the overall "color" of your document is to adjust tabs and indention, thereby adding or reducing white space at the beginning of each line.

Often, tabs and indents appropriate for word-processed manuscripts are too deep for narrower columns, particularly if a different typeface or type size has been chosen.

To adjust the amount of indention at the beginnings of paragraphs,

Type: SHFT F8 (**FORMAT**)

Select: Option 1 (**LINE**)

Select: Option 8 (**TAB SPACING**)

Response: You'll see a ruler showing the half-inch default spacing for tabs.

Type: (HOME) (HOME) Left Cursor Control Key

This moves your cursor to the left-hand margin of the page.

Type: (CTRL) (END) (**DELETE TO END OF LINE**) (to eliminate all existing tabs.)

Type: Advance the cursor to the position where you want to place a tab.

Type: L (at each position where you want a tab to appear.)

Type: (RETURN) (RETURN) (to return to the editing screen.)

Adjusting White Space within and at the End of Lines

Your choice of hyphenation also influences the "color" of your documents. This is true whether you're placing text in flush-left/ragged-right or justified columns. With hyphenation, words that are too long to fit comfortably on one line are broken between syllables and set on two lines. Although most often used with justified text, hyphenation is an equally important tool for flush-left/ragged-right text.

Compare the examples below:

> sleeping puppy. We observed the brownish fox jumping happily around the sleeping puppy. We observed the brownish fox jumping happily around the

> around the sleeping puppy. We observed the brownish fox jumping happily around the sleeping puppy. We observed the brownish fox jumping happily around the

We observed the brownish fox jumping happily around the sleeping puppy. We observed the brownish fox jumping happily around the sleeping puppy. We

observed the brownish fox jumping happily around the sleeping puppy. We observed the brownish fox jumping happily around the sleep-

You can see that activating WordPerfect's **HYPHENATION** feature eliminates the large gaps of white space at the end of flush-left/ragged-right lines. Likewise, **HYPHENATION** eliminates unnatural word spacing that occurs within lines of justified type—especially short lines of text set in a large type size.

To activate **HYPHENATION**,

Type: SHFT F8 (**FORMAT**)

Select: Option 1 (**LINE**)

Select: Option 1 (**HYPHENATION**)

Response: Alternatives include:

Option 1 (**OFF**)
Option 2 (**MANUAL**)
Option 3 (**AUTO**)

Select: Option 3 (**AUTO**)

WordPerfect automatically will hyphenate words that are too long to fit on one line.

If you had chosen Option 2 (**MANUAL**), WordPerfect would stop at the end of each line and ask you to manually hyphenate words that were too long to fit on the line.

207

Type: (RETURN) (RETURN)

This returns you to your editing screen.

Adjusting the Hyphenation Zone

By adjusting the **HYPHENATION ZONE**, you can increase or decrease the number of words that will be hyphenated. Words that begin before or after the **HYPHENATION ZONE** are automatically hyphenated (or manually hyphenated). Words that begin after the left side of the **HYPHENATION ZONE** and extend past the right side of the **HYPHENATION ZONE** are moved in their entirety to the next line.

By adjusting the width of the zone, you can control the number of words that will be hyphenated:

- A narrower zone increases the number of hyphenated words.
- A wider zone reduces hyphenation.

To adjust the **HYPHENATION ZONE**,

Type: SHFT F8 (**FORMAT**)

Select: Option 1 (**LINE**)

Select: Option 2 (**HYPHENATION ZONE**)

Response: Left 10%
Right 4%

To reduce hyphenation, increase the **HYPHENATION ZONE**.

Type: 12

Type: (RETURN)

Response: This replaces the **10%** default with a **12%** setting and advances your cursor to the right setting.

Type: 6

Type: (RETURN)

Response: This replaces the **4%** default with a **6%** figure.

The **HYPHENATION ZONE** is now wider. To return to your editing screen,

Type: (RETURN) (RETURN)

To create a narrower **HYPHENATION ZONE**, which often improves the appearance of flush-left/ragged-right columns,

Type: SHFT F8 (**FORMAT**)

Select: Option 1 (**LINE**)

Select: Option 2 (**HYPHENATION ZONE**)

Response: Left 10%
Right 4%

To increase hyphenation, reduce the **HYPHENATION ZONE**.

Type: 8

Type: (RETURN)

Response: This replaces the **10%** default with an **8%** setting and advances your cursor to the right setting.

Type: 3

Type: (RETURN)

Response: This replaces the **4%** default with a **3%** figure.

The **HYPHENATION ZONE** is now narrower, which means more words will be split between lines. To return to your editing screen,

Type: (RETURN) (RETURN)

Modifying Justification Limits

WordPerfect also allows you to modify justification limits—the minimum or maximum amount of space between words when lines are justified (or of equal length). Because this affects the density of words per line, it influences publication "color."

With WordPerfect, you can adjust justification limits in the following ways:

- Word spacing can be compressed from **0%** to **100%**. The default is **75%**.

- Word spacing can be expanded from **100%** to **unlimited**. The default is **400%**.

To adjust word-spacing justification limits,

Select: SHFT F8 (**FORMAT**)

Select: Option 4 (**OTHER**)

Select: Option 6 (**PRINTER FUNCTIONS**)

Select: Option 4 (**WORD SPACING JUSTIFICATION LIMITS**)

Response: Compressed to (0% - 100%) 60% (This is the compression default. If you accept it, word spacing will never be less than 60 percent of ideal.)

Type: Any value between **0%** and **100%.**

Type: (RETURN)

Smaller numbers indicate that, when necessary, the spaces between words will be reduced to accommodate justification. The disadvantage of smaller numbers is that the spacing can be tightened to the point that the words run together to achieve justification, making your publication difficult to read. Larger numbers "open up" a document by forcing more space between words.

Response: Expanded to (100% - unlimited) 400%

Type: Any value between **100%** and **400%**.

The value for normal word spacing is 100 percent. As you enter larger numbers, more and more space between words is added when necessary to justify the lines. However, extra space can become visually distracting and create unsightly "rivers" of white space running through your publication.

Eliminating Widows and Orphans

The appearance and credibility of your document can be enhanced by WordPerfect's ability to automatically eliminate widows and orphans, described earlier in this chapter. To activate WordPerfect's **WIDOW/ORPHAN** feature,

Type: SHFT F8 (**FORMAT**)

Select: Option 1 (**LINE**)

Select: Option 9 (**WIDOW/ORPHAN PROTECTION**)

Response: The blinking cursor under the **N** in **No** indicates that **WIDOW/ORPHAN PROTECTION** has not been activated.

Type: Y

Type: (RETURN) (RETURN)

Response: You're returned to the editing screen. **WIDOW/ORPHAN PROTECTION** will be in effect from the cursor location forward.

Rotating Text

If you use a PostScript printer, you can rotate text. By taking a line of type and rotating it 90 degrees, for example, you can stand it on its head, so that it runs up the side of your page. Or, you can rotate the text 180 degrees so that the line appears upside down. This technique can come in handy when preparing a horizontal address panel for the back of a three-panel brochure.

Text rotation requires the use of boxes. Let's start by creating a new graphics box for this example.

Select: ALT F9 (**GRAPHICS**)

Select: Option 4 (**USER-DEFINED BOX**)

Select: Option 1 (**CREATE**)

Select: Option 3 (**TYPE**)

Select: Option 2 (**PAGE**)

Select: Option 4 (**VERTICAL POSITION**)

Select: Option 1 (**FULL PAGE**)

Select: Option 5 (**HORIZONTAL POSITION**)

Select: Option 1 (**MARGINS**)

Select: Option 1 (**LEFT**)

Select: Option 6 (**SIZE**)

Select: Option 3 (**BOTH WIDTH AND HEIGHT**)

Response: Width = 6.5" (This figure depends both on the margins as well as the measuring system you've chosen.)

Type: 2

Type: (RETURN)

Response: Height = 9"

Type: (RETURN)

Select: Option 8 (**EDIT**)

Now that the size and placement of the box have been determined, select a typeface, type size and type style for a headline and enter the words.

Type: CTRL F8 (**FONT**)

Select: Option 4 (**BASE FONT**)

Type: Scroll down until **HELVETICA** is highlighted.

Type: (RETURN)

Response: Point size: 10

Type: 36

Type: (RETURN)

Type: Graphic excellence can be yours!

Type: (RETURN)

To rotate the type and place it vertically on the page,

Type: ALT F9 (**GRAPHICS**)

Response: Option 1 (**0 /degree symbol/**)
Option 2 (**90 /degree symbol/**)
Option 3 (**180 /degree symbol/**)
Option 4 (**270 /degree symbol/**)

Select: Option 2 (**90 /degree symbol/**)

Type: F7 (**EXIT**)

Type: (RETURN) (RETURN)

The result should be similar to the illustration on the next page:

Graphic excellence can be yours!

Creating a Reversed Headline

A new generation of color printers is on the horizon. In anticipation of their appearance, WordPerfect allows you to "mix" ink colors to create the exact shade and intensity you want.

However, until low-cost color printers become available, you can use this feature to create shaded type—or even reversed type (white words against a black background or dark gray background). Reversed type can add drama and impact to your documents by making your headline stand out from others on the same page.

Creating a reversed headline with a PostScript printer involves four steps. (Instructions for each step follow.)

1. Changing the default for **USER-DEFINED BOX** from a white background to a black background.

2. Creating a **USER-DEFINED BOX** in the proper position on the page.

3. Centering the headline, selecting the appropriate typeface, type size, type style and entering the text of the headline.

4. Changing the color of the headline text to white, so it will stand out against the black background of the **USER-DEFINED BOX**.

Remember that a **USER-DEFINED BOX** won't appear in a compiled list of figures, text or tables.

TIP: You may change the **USER-DEFINED BOX** option from white to black *before* you create the box. You may also create the box first, then change the option from white to black. Be sure that in **REVEAL CODES** your cursor is placed on or before your box and not after it.

WordPerfect's **REVEAL CODES** command (ALT F3) can be very useful in helping you locate the precise position for making those changes.

Although some of the following steps are repetitive, you will not only learn how to create a reversed headline, but also will review many important WordPerfect commands used in creating boxes and manipulating type.

Step One: Changing the Default for User-defined Boxes

The first step is to change the background of the next **USER-DEFINED BOX** you create to solid black.

Type: ALT F9 (**GRAPHICS**)

Select: Option 4 (**USER-DEFINED BOX**)

Select: Option 4 (**OPTIONS**)

Select: Option 9 (**GRAY SHADING (% OF BLACK)**)

Response: 0%

Type: 100

Type: (RETURN)

This creates a totally black reversed box. (Choose 75 percent if you want a dark gray background. As you choose smaller percentages, the background shade becomes lighter.)

Step Two: Placing the Box

Next, place the **USER-DEFINED BOX** where you want your reversed headline to appear. Let's assume you want the headline to be centered in a black box three inches deep that spans the top of your publication. To create the box,

Type:	ALT F9 (**GRAPHICS**)
Select:	Option 4 (**USER-DEFINED BOX**)
Select:	Option 1 (**CREATE**)
Select:	Option 3 (**TYPE**)
Select:	Option 2 (**PAGE**)

This "locks" the box to a specific point on a specific page, instead of having it "float" with surrounding text.

Select:	Option 5 (**HORIZONTAL POSITION**)
Select:	Option 1 (**MARGINS**)
Select:	Option 4 (**BOTH LEFT AND RIGHT**)

This is WordPerfect's way of creating a box that extends from one margin to the other.

Select:	Option 6 (**SIZE**)
Response:	You're presented with the following alternatives:

Option 1 **WIDTH (AUTO HEIGHT)**
Option 2 **HEIGHT (AUTO WIDTH)**
Option 3 **BOTH WIDTH AND HEIGHT**

Select: Option 3 (**BOTH WIDTH AND HEIGHT**)

Response: Width = 6.5"

The width of the box is established by the page margins. The use of inches is based on the measuring system you've previously chosen.

Type: (RETURN)

Response: Height = 6.5"

Type: 3

Type: (RETURN)

Type: (RETURN)

This returns you to your editing screen.

Step Three: Adding Headline Words

Now it's time to place the reversed words within the black box you've created. Position your cursor before the **USER-DEFINED BOX** code using the **REVEAL CODES** command (ALT F3).

Type: ALT F9 (**GRAPHICS**)

Select: Option 4 (**USER-DEFINED BOX**)

Select: Option 2 (**EDIT**)

Response: User-defined box Number: 2 (or one number higher than the last **USER-DEFINED BOX** created so far.)

Type: 1 (or the appropriate number of the reversed **USER-DEFINED BOX** you've just created.)

Type: (RETURN)

Select: Option 8 (**EDIT**)

Any words you now type will be placed in the reversed **USER-DEFINED BOX** you've just created. Before you enter the words that will be contained in your reversed headline box, enter the font codes that correspond to the appropriate typeface, type size and type style.

Type: CTRL F8 (**FONT**)

Select: Option 4 (**BASE FONT**)

Response: You're presented with an alphabetical list of all available resident and downloaded fonts.

Type: Scroll down until **BOLD HELVETICA** is highlighted.

Type: (RETURN)

Response: Type size: 10 (or the last type size chosen.)

Type: 36

Type: (RETURN)

Type: CTRL F8 (**FONT**)

Select: Option 5 (**PRINT COLOR**)

Select: Option 2 (**WHITE**)

Type: (RETURN)

Type: Reversed headlines add impact to your publications!

Before moving on, however, let's break the headline into three lines by entering (**RETURN**) immediately after the word **headlines** and deleting the space before **add**.

Likewise, enter (**RETURN**) immediately after the word **to** and delete the space before **your**.

Return to the beginning of the headline.

Type: ALT F4 (**BLOCK**)

Move the cursor to the end of the headline.

Type: SHFT F6 (**CENTER**)

Response: (Cntr)? (Y/N) No

Type: Y

These steps ensure that the headline will be properly centered. Your screen now should look like this:

The next step is to center the headline vertically within the reversed box. The headline then will be surrounded by equal amounts of space above and below it.

Type: (HOME) (HOME) Up Cursor Control Key (This returns the cursor to the beginning of the headline text.)

Type: SHFT F8 (**FORMAT**)

Select: Option 2 (**PAGE**)

Select: Option 1 (**CENTER PAGE (TOP TO BOTTOM)**))

Response: No

Type: Y

Type: (RETURN)

The headline now is set up to be both vertically and horizontally centered within the reversed box. The final step is to change the normally black type to white type, so that it will form a dramatic contrast against its black background.

Step Four: Creating White Type

Now we come to the crucial step in creating a reversed headline. With the cursor still on the first letter of the headline,

Type: CTRL F8 (**FONT**)

Select: Option 5 (**PRINT COLOR**)

Response: You're presented with WordPerfect's **PRINT COLOR** menu.

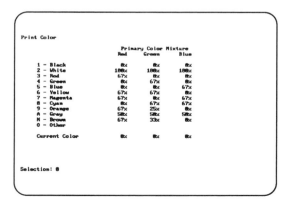

Select: Option 2 (**WHITE**)

Type: (RETURN) (RETURN)

Type: F7 (**EXIT**)

Type: (RETURN)

This returns you to your editing screen.

Use WordPerfect's **VIEW DOCUMENT** command (SHFT F7, 6). Depending upon your monitor, you might see only a black box. But if you **PRINT** the page (SHFT F7, 2), you'll find that your words appear in white against a black background! The headline should look like this:

Because you'll be returning to the example later in this chapter, save it. You'll use it again when you experiment with improving the appearance of this headline.

Type: F10 (**SAVE**)

Response: Document to be saved:

Type: REVHEAD

Type: (RETURN)

Returning User-defined Boxes to White Background

To return to normal **USER-DEFINED BOX**es with white backgrounds, repeat the steps used to change the background to black, with the exception of the last step. Specifically,

Type: ALT 9 (**GRAPHICS**)

Select: Option 4 (**USER-DEFINED BOX**)

Select: Option 4 (**OPTIONS**)

Select: Option 9 (**GRAY SHADING (% OF BLACK)**)

Response: 100 0% (selected above)

Type: 0

Type: (RETURN)

Response: **USER-DEFINED BOX**es, once again, will be created with no borders and a white background.

Creating Shaded Type

Shaded type can add two-color impact to your publications at a one-color price. Shaded type is particularly valuable when used to create large, bold, sans-serif headlines, consisting of a few words surrounded by lots of white space.

To create shaded text,

Type: CTRL F8 (**FONT**)

Select:	Option 5 (**PRINT COLOR**)
Select:	Option O (**OTHER**)
Response:	The cursor jumps to the **0%** under **Red**.
Type:	60
Type:	(RETURN)
Response:	The cursor jumps to the **0%** under **Green**.
Type:	60
Type:	(RETURN)
Response:	The cursor jumps to the **0%** under **Blue**.
Type:	60
Type:	(RETURN)
Type:	CTRL F8 (**FONT**)
Select:	Option 4 (**BASE FONT**)
Response:	A list of all available resident and downloadable fonts. Scroll down until you reach **HELVETICA BOLD**.
Type:	(RETURN)
Response:	Type size: 10 (or last type size chosen.)
Type:	24
Type:	(RETURN)
Type:	Exciting Headlines
Type:	(RETURN)

This returns you to your editing screen. When printed, your page should be similar to the illustration below:

Exciting Headlines

Shaded type can range from very dark to very light. When printed, type appears darker as the "percentage" approaches 100. Type appears lighter as the "percentage" approaches 0. In most cases, you'll probably vary shadings at 20 percent intervals.

Shaded type can be particularly attractive when used in conjunction with shaded boxes. As the examples below show, interesting effects can be achieved by placing light gray type in a dark gray box, or dark gray type in a light gray box.

ONE DAY SALE

ONE DAY SALE

Moving On

This chapter introduced you to many of the tips and tricks of typography.

Great advances are being made in this area. It pays to stay up to date as WordPerfect continues to enhance its ability to accurately place and fine-tune text.

Many of the steps described in Chapter Six and in this chapter involve entering long sequences of keystrokes that might have to be frequently repeated in a long document (e.g., a book containing numerous reversed headlines).

In Chapter Eight, you'll see how WordPerfect's powerful **STYLE** command (ALT F8) can help you reduce these complicated keyboard sequences. In Chapter Nine, you'll learn how WordPerfect's powerful **MACRO** command (ALT F10) can expedite page formatting and layout of your document.

8

Using Stylesheets for Consistency and Speed

Consistency of style is an important goal when producing print communications. Consistent type treatments, letter and line spacing, and page formatting improve the appearance and effectiveness of your projects.

For example, typeface, type size and type style options should be consistent throughout your publication, particularly in the following areas:

- Headlines
- Kickers (short phrases that introduce headlines)
- Bylines (authors' credits)
- Subheads
- Body copy
- Jumplines (e.g., "Continued on page 38" and "Continued from page 29")
- Captions
- Header and footer information (e.g., publication title, section or chapter divisions, author's name, page numbers)
- Footnotes and endnotes

WordPerfect's **STYLE** command (ALT F8) makes consistency easy. By using **STYLE**s you can create stylesheets, containing your choice of type characteristics, as well as alignment and line spacing.

You even can include sophisticated typographic refinements, such as kerning, shading, word and letter spacing, and precise adjustments of margins, tabs and hyphenation zones in the **STYLE**s you create. These settings can be stored as separate files and accessed as needed. That minimizes the chances of choosing the wrong type characteristics or entering an inconsistent setting.

More important, if you're producing a series of advertisements, books, brochures, newsletters or training materials, WordPerfect's **STYLE**s can be re-used, making it easy to achieve consistency throughout a series.

It's important to note that WordPerfect's powerful **STYLE** command can be used any time, even while you're writing or editing your document.

A Shortcut to Achieving Consistent Design

If properly used, WordPerfect's **STYLE** command can save you a lot of time. Complicated sequences of keystrokes can be reduced to simple files, accessed quickly and easily. For example, instead of using a series of "selection" sequences, accessed from the **FONT** (CTRL F8), **STYLE** (ALT F8), **FORMAT** (SHFT F8) and **CENTER** (SHFT F6) commands each time you want to change from body copy to headline type and back again, WordPerfect's **STYLE** command lets you instantly invoke the desired keyboard command sequences.

Finally, because **STYLE**s can be edited, you quickly can make major revisions throughout your publication by simply changing the **STYLE** definition. That's a lot faster than reformatting every headline, subhead and caption.

As you grow accustomed to WordPerfect's **STYLE** command, you'll wonder how you ever did without it!

Creating a Style

Let's create a **STYLE** that determines headline treatment for a newsletter.

Type: ALT F8 (**STYLE**)

Response: The **STYLE** menu is displayed.

Select: Option 3 (**CREATE**)

Select: Option 1 (**NAME**)

Type: MAINHEAD

Type: (RETURN)

You can include up to eleven letters in a **STYLE**'s name, which should relate logically to its function. As you become comfortable using **STYLE**s, you'll undoubtedly come up with your own "shorthand" for naming them. The name will appear first in the listing of **STYLE**s when you execute the **STYLE** command and the **REVEAL CODES** command (ALT F3).

Select: Option 2 (**TYPE**)

Response: You're given two options:
Option 1 (**PAIRED**)
Option 2 (**OPEN**)

You'll probably use Option 1 (**PAIRED**) more often than Option 2 (**OPEN**). **PAIRED STYLE**s are used for selected word groups—headlines, subheads, body copy or captions—which have a distinct beginning and end. **PAIRED STYLE**s can be turned on and off at will.

When you select Option 2 (**OPEN**), the **STYLE** remains active throughout the rest of your publication. **OPEN STYLE**s usually are used to establish formats, such as margins, that will be maintained throughout the publication.

Select: Option 1 (**PAIRED**)

Select: Option 3 (**DESCRIPTION**)

You can use as many as 59 characters to define the purpose and use of this **STYLE**. The **DESCRIPTION** feature is there to remind you of the intended use of the **STYLE**. It also can be used to remind you of the kind of project a particular **STYLE** has been assigned (e.g., customer newsletter, employee handbook, etc.).

Type: Defines newsletter headline treatment.

Type: (RETURN)

Select: Option 4 (**CODES**)

Now you define the typeface, type size, type style, alignment and line spacing—or any other formatting options—that you want for your newsletter headlines. This section can be as lengthy as necessary to accommodate all your typographic refinements described in the previous chapter. (However, let's make this example relatively short.)

Response: The screen divides in half, with a box containing the words, **Place Style On Codes above, and Style Off Codes below**.

This lets you choose the type alternatives you want your **STYLE** to define when activated, as well as the type choices you want when you turn off the **STYLE**.

To help you visualize this better, notice how the **CODES** screen is divided in half and the **REVEAL CODES** command (ALT F3) is activated automatically.

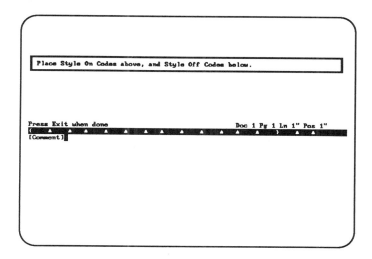

Use your cursor control keys to switch between the **STYLE ON** and **STYLE OFF** formatting codes.

Type: CTRL F8 (**FONT**)

Select: Option 4 (**BASE FONT**)

Response: You're presented with a list of all typefaces, type sizes and type styles currently available with the selected printer. Options include resident fonts, downloaded fonts and—if you're using an HP-compatible printer—font cartridges. If you're using a PostScript printer, for example, scroll down the list until you come to **HELVETICA**.

Type: (RETURN) (to accept this choice.)

Response: Point Size: (Type in point size.)

Type: 24

Type: (RETURN)

231

You also can define the placement and line spacing of the headline at this point. For example, if you want to center the headline,

Type: SHFT F6 (**CENTER**)

If you want the headline double-spaced,

Type: SHFT F8 (**FORMAT**)

Select: Option 1 (**LINE**)

Response: The screen displays the **FORMAT: LINE** menu.

Select: Option 6 (**LINE SPACING**)

Response: The blinking cursor highlights the currently active default, in this case, **1**.

Type: 2

Type: (RETURN)

This replaces the default single-line spacing with a double-line spacing.

When you've finished formatting headline type characteristics and line spacing, enter the formatting choices for text when the **STYLE** is deactivated.

When you're satisfied with your choices,

Type: F7 (**EXIT**)

Response: This returns you to the **STYLES: EDIT** menu.

The final step in creating a **STYLE** is to define the purpose of the (**RETURN**) key when using the **PAIRED STYLE** mode.

Select: Option 5 (**ENTER**)

Response: Option 1 (**HRT**)

Option 2 (**OFF**)
Option 3 (**OFF/ON**)

Option 1 (**HRT**) doesn't affect the function of the (**RETURN**) key, which operates as a normal hard return. It doesn't affect the way the stylesheet performs.

Option 2 (**OFF**) lets you use the (**RETURN**) key to turn off the **STYLE** definition.

Option 3 (**OFF/ON**) allows you to use the (**RETURN**) key as a toggle to turn the **STYLE** on and off.

Select: Option 2 (**OFF**)

To end the style creation process,

Type: F7 F7 (**EXIT**)   (Press F7 twice.)

Creating Styles by Example

You also can create a **STYLE** by using WordPerfect's **BLOCK** command (ALT F4). Start by highlighting a previously formatted group of words. This can save you time, because you can easily replicate a format that took a lot of trial and error until it appeared just right.

Type: ALT F4 (**BLOCK**)

Use your left/right cursor control keys to choose the formatted words you want saved as a **STYLE**. Remember that (**CTRL**) right and (**CTRL**) left cursor control keys advance the cursor one word at a time. When the passage you want saved as a formatted **STYLE** has been highlighted,

Type: ALT F8 (**STYLE**)

Select: Option 3 (**CREATE**)

Select: Option 1 (**NAME**)

Type: SUBHEAD

Type: (RETURN)

Select: Option 3 (**DESCRIPTION**)

Type: Provides headline/body copy transition

Type: (RETURN)

To return to editing your document,

Type: F7 (**EXIT**)

Applying Styles as You Write New Text

STYLEs can be applied while you're writing or editing. To apply **STYLE**s as you write,

Type: ALT F8 (**STYLE**)

Response: You're presented with an alphabetical listing of the **STYLE**s you've previously created.

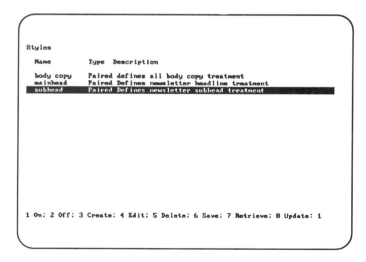

```
Styles

  Name           Type   Description

  body copy      Paired defines all body copy treatment
  mainhead       Paired Defines newsletter headline treatment
  subhead        Paired Defines newsletter subhead treatment




1 On; 2 Off; 3 Create; 4 Edit; 5 Delete; 6 Save; 7 Retrieve; 8 Update: 1
```

Type: Use your up/down cursor control keys until you've high-lighted the **STYLE** you want to use for the next group of words. In this case, **MAINHEAD**.

Select: Option 1 (**ON**)

Type: WordPerfect's Styles Save Time!

Type: ALT F8 (**STYLE**)

Select: Option 2 (**OFF**)

To continue the example,

Type: ALT F8 (**STYLE**)

Type: Scroll down until the **SUBHEAD STYLE** is highlighted.

Select: Option 1 (**ON**)

Type: And they're easy to apply.

Type: ALT F8 (**STYLE**)

Select: Option 2 (**OFF**)

Use WordPerfect's **VIEW DOCUMENT** (SHFT F7, 6) or **PRINT** (SHFT F7, 2) commands to see how the **STYLE**s formatted your words.

Applying Styles to Previously Entered Text

You also can apply **STYLE**s while editing your text. Start by placing the cursor at the beginning of a word group that you want to format, using a previously created **STYLE**.

Type: ALT F4 (**BLOCK**)

Type: Use the right cursor control key, or (**CTRL**) right cursor control key, to select the letters or words you want to format.

Type: ALT F8 (**STYLE**)

Response: You're presented with an alphabetical list of previously created **STYLE**s.

Type: Use your down cursor control key to advance to the **STYLE** you want to apply to the highlighted words.

Select: Option 1 (**ON**)

Response: The words are formatted and you return to your editing screen.

Editing a Style

If you want to modify the appearance of your publication by changing previously chosen typeface, type size, type style or alignment alternatives, you easily can edit a **STYLE**. You also might want to edit a **STYLE** if you've purchased new downloadable fonts that you want to substitute for previously chosen typefaces.

Editing lets you quickly change typeface, type size, type style or alignment formats throughout the document. By editing the **STYLE**, you automatically can modify the appearance of every word, or group of words, to which the **STYLE** relates. With a few simple keystrokes, you can make major changes in the appearance of your document.

To edit a previously chosen **STYLE**,

Type: ALT F8 (**STYLE**)

Response: You're presented with an alphabetical list of previously defined **STYLE**s.

Type: Use your down cursor control key to highlight the **STYLE** you want to edit.

Select: Option 4 (**EDIT**)

Response: You're presented with the name, description, codes and **(RETURN)** key options for the **STYLE** you've chosen. Although you can edit the name or description, in most cases you'll probably want to edit the codes.

Select: Option 4 (**CODES**)

Response: Notice how WordPerfect's **REVEAL CODES** command (ALT F3) automatically is activated to help you.

Type: Make your editing changes. When you're finished,

Type: F7 F7 F7 (**EXIT**) (Press **F7** three times.)

That returns you to your editing screen and changes the formatting of all word groups to which the **STYLE** relates.

Deleting a Style

You can delete a **STYLE**. You might want to do so because a format doesn't look good when printed or relates to a downloadable font you no longer want to use.

You also may want to delete a **STYLE** that's unique to a single document and doesn't belong in a **STYLE** library you're creating for several different publications (see below).

To delete a previously defined **STYLE**,

Type: ALT F8 (**STYLE**)

Response: You're presented with an alphabetical list of previously defined **STYLE**s.

Type: Use your down cursor control key to highlight the **STYLE** you want to delete.

Select: Option 5 (**DELETE**)

Response: Delete Style?   (Y/N) No

Type: Y

Type: (RETURN)

You'll return to your editing screen. To verify that the **STYLE** has been deleted,

Type: ALT F8 (**STYLE**)

Response: The deleted **STYLE** shouldn't appear in the listing of available **STYLE**s.

TIP: This act is irrevocable. You can't retrieve a deleted **STYLE**.

Creating a Style Library

STYLEs normally are saved with the document for which they've been designed. It's possible, however, to create **STYLE** libraries, which let **STYLE**s created for one publication be used again for other publications.

To create a **STYLE** library,

Type: ALT F8 (**STYLE**)

Response: You're presented with an alphabetical list of previously defined **STYLE**s.

Select: Option 6 (**SAVE**)

Response: You're prompted to enter a filename. Let's assume you want to re-use the **STYLE**s in future newsletters.

Type: NEWSTYLS

Type: (RETURN)

To avoid confusion, choose a "shorthand" filename that explains the contents of the file in just eight letters.

To return to text entry and editing,

Type: F7 (**EXIT**)

Retrieving a Style Library

Later, when you're working on a different document and want to use a previously defined **STYLE** library,

Type: ALT F8 (**STYLE**)

Response: The **STYLE**s menu appears without any defined **STYLE**s.

Type: Option 7 (**RETRIEVE**)

Response: Filename:

Type: The name of your previously stored **STYLE** library (in this case, **NEWSTYLS**).

Type: (RETURN)

Response: The **STYLE** menu now displays an alphabetical list of **STYLE**s created for your original document that now are available with your current document.

TIP: You might want to create a **STYLE** library in a separate sub-directory. When retrieving a previously stored **STYLE** library, you have to enter its full pathname (e.g., **\STYLIB\NEW-STYLS**).

Other Uses for Styles

In addition to using **STYLE**s to establish typographic formats, they also can be used to create page layouts. Let's create an **OPEN** style, which features a page layout for a three-column newsletter.

Type: ALT F8 (**STYLE**)

Select: Option 3 (**CREATE**)

Select: Option 1 (**NAME**)

239

Type: 3COLGRID

Type: (RETURN)

Select: Option 2 (**TYPE**)

Response: Option 1 (**PAIRED**)
Option 2 (**OPEN**)

Select: Option 2 (**OPEN**)

Select: Option 3 (**DESCRIPTION**)

Type: Creates three-column newsletter grid

Type: (RETURN)

Select: Option 4 (**CODES**)

Type: ALT F7 (**MATH/COLUMNS**)

Select: Option 4 (**COLUMN DEF**)

Response: You're presented with the **TEXT COLUMN** definition menu. Accept the **NEWSPAPER** format, as described in Chapter Three.

Select: Option 2 (**NUMBER OF COLUMNS**)

Response: The cursor under **2** will blink.

Type: 3

Type: (RETURN)

This replaces the default two-column format with a three-column format.

Response: Notice how the column widths are computed automatically.

Type: (RETURN)

The final step in activating the three-column format is as follows:

Select: Option 3 (**COLUMN ON/OFF**)

The three-column format now is saved. In a similar way, you can save **STYLE**s that define margins, create headers and footers, assign page number locations, center title pages and customize page layouts in numerous other ways.

Moving On

In Chapter Nine, you'll look more closely at the way macros and stylesheets can work together with WordPerfect's desktop publishing tools to help you create good-looking publications. You'll also examine how desktop publishing features work with other hardware and software options, such as the WordPerfect Library and expanded memory boards.

9

Advanced Techniques

By now you're familiar with WordPerfect's basic desktop publishing tools and how they interact.

To review, desktop publishing with WordPerfect is based on a combination of six major features introduced in Version 5.0:

1) The ability to create and accurately locate boxes for placing text and graphics files created with other programs, as well as for controlling white space.

2) The ability to control the placement of text on a page, including mixing multiple typefaces, sizes and styles.

3) The use of macros and **STYLE**s to expedite page layout and select and change type characteristics.

4) Organizational capabilities, such as generating automatic references, endnotes, footnotes, index entries and tables of contents, as well as detailed lists of graphs, drawings, tables and illustrations.

5) A page preview feature that lets you view your work on your computer screen at varying degrees of magnification.

6) An enhanced **REVEAL CODES** feature that allows on-screen editing and formatting.

To move beyond basic desktop publishing, let's look at advanced macros, which let you assemble those features into quick routines that establish page layouts, add graphic accents and choose type attributes.

Creating a Chained Macro

WordPerfect lets you *chain* macros. As the word "chain" implies, macros can be created that include—or link together—other previously created macros.

For example, in earlier chapters, you learned how to use macros to create a border, a multi-column page layout and boxes of various sizes. In Chapter Eight, you examined **STYLE**s and their use in selecting a given typeface, type size and type style.

Macros and **STYLE**s can be chained together to operate in sequence automatically. Thus, by executing one macro, you simultaneously can

- Add page borders
- Add white space
- Establish multi-column layouts
- Choose a particular typeface, type size and type style

You can even use repeating macros to lay out a multi-page newsletter automatically, complete with page numbers alternating on the left- and right-hand pages. Let's go through a sample exercise to see how macros and **STYLE**s can be placed within "master" macros.

Assume you want to create a macro that will lay out the first page of a newsletter and that you've already created several individual macros that perform the functions described. Even if you haven't created the macros that are the component parts of this "master" macro, you'll see how easy it is to chain macros together.

Start by opening a previously stored practice document that includes several prepared macros and **STYLE**s.

Type: CTRL F10 (**MACRO DEFINE**)

Response: You're prompted to name the macro.

Type: NEWSPG1

Type: (RETURN)

Response: You're prompted to describe the macro.

Type: Creates front page of 3-col newsletter

Type: (RETURN)

Response: The **MACRO DEF** prompt indicates that the following keystrokes will be recorded.

It's important to note that WordPerfect's macro creation feature can only add one chained macro at a time. Thus, when creating the following master macro, save the macro and reopen it each time you add a chained macro.

Type: ALT F10 (**MACRO**)

Response: Macro:

You're prompted to name a previously prepared macro you want to include in the macro you're currently creating.

Type: MASTHEAD

Type: (RETURN)

The above assumes that you've created a graphics box that automatically imports a file containing a newsletter masthead or nameplate (previously created with a draw-type program).

Type: ALT F10 (**MACRO**)

Response: Macro:

Again, you're asked to enter the name of the previously created macro.

Type: BOTMBORD

Type: (RETURN)

This is the name of a macro that places a quarter-inch line along the bottom of the page.

Type: ALT F10 (**MACRO**)

Response: Again, you're prompted to enter the name of a previously created macro.

Type: 3COLFMT

Type: (RETURN)

This previously created macro creates three columns on a page and turns on the column-formatting feature.

Type: ALT F10 (**MACRO**)

Response: Again, you're prompted to enter the name of a previously created macro.

Type: VERTPG1

Type: (RETURN)

This refers to a macro that places vertical lines between the columns that extend from the bottom of the page up to the masthead.

Type: ALT F8 (**STYLE**)

Response: You're shown an alphabetical list of all available **STYLE**s.

Type: Use your up/down cursor control keys until the **STYLE** you want to use is highlighted.

Type: (RETURN)

Type: F7 (**EXIT**)

At this point, you've completed both laying out the front page and selecting type. To end the macro,

Type: CTRL F10 (**MACRO DEFINE**)

This concludes the macro creation process. You're returned to your editing screen.

In a similar way, you can create macros for each page in your newsletter. You might create separate macros for left- and right-hand pages in order to alternate header and footer information. These macros could be called **RTNEWSPG** and **LFTNEWPG**.

Using a Chained Macro

To quickly lay out the front page of your newsletter with the chained macro,

Type: ALT F10 (**MACRO**)

Response: Macro:

Type: NEWSPG1

Type: (RETURN)

Response: All the chained macros included above will be applied in the order they were entered. The result will be a formatted page ready for your words.

Editing a Macro

There may be occasions when you'll want to change your macro definition. You might find that the vertical lines extend into the masthead box or that a different column layout is needed. WordPerfect makes it easy to edit previously created macros.

Type: CTRL F10 (**MACRO DEFINE**)

Response: Define macro:

This prompts you to enter the macro name. For purposes of illustration, let's enter the name of the macro created above.

Type: NEWSPG1

Type: (RETURN)

Response: NEWSPG1.WPM Is Already Defined.   1 Replace; 2 Edit: 0

Select: Option 2 (**EDIT**)

Response: You're presented with the **MACRO: EDIT** screen, which lists the filename and two options.

Option 1 (**DESCRIPTION**) lets you change your description of the macro.

Option 2 (**ACTION**) lets you eliminate macros that have been included or add new macros, **STYLE**s or keystrokes.

Select: Option 2 (**ACTION**)

Response: The cursor advances to the box, which you can edit using your left/right cursor control keys.

Notice how this **MACRO: EDIT** box is similar to WordPerfect's **REVEAL CODES** (ALT F3) screen.

Make whatever changes you want in the macro. When you're finished,

Type: F7 (**EXIT**)

Type: (RETURN)

You now are returned to the editing screen. The macro you've edited has been revised and saved.

Repeating a Macro

WordPerfect's **MACRO** feature makes it easy to create multiple page layouts. Macros can be set up to repeat as many times as you want. The **ESCAPE** key (ESC) is used to repeat macros automatically.

Using the above example, let's say that within a macro you want to repeat another macro six times. Before you press **ALT F10** to enter the macro into the chain, press the **ESCAPE** key.

Response: Repeat Value = 8

   Type: The number of times you want to repeat the following macro.

   Type: ALT F10 (**MACRO**)

   Type: The name of the macro you want repeated.

   Type: (RETURN)

   Type: CTRL F10 (**MACRO DEFINE**)

   This ends the macro creation process. When the macro is invoked, the chained macro inside is repeated as many times as you've indicated.

Sharing Macros with Other Documents

Unlike **STYLE**s, macros are stored in separate files, independent of the document in which they were created. Thus, macros can be shared with more than one document without having to go through the saving and retrieving process required when **STYLE**s are shared.

WordPerfect macros are easily identified by their **.WPM** suffix. However, you can use WordPerfect's **SETUP** command (SHFT F1, 7, 3) to identify a previously created subdirectory where all macros are stored.

Creating Compound Documents

As you begin to create sophisticated publications with Word-Perfect, you'll find yourself placing a previously written file inside your current document. WordPerfect's **RETRIEVE TEXT** command (SHFT F10) lets you do this without destroying your original file. Thus, when you edit the retrieved file within your current document, the original file remains intact. (Of course, any changes you make won't appear in the original file.)

To retrieve a previously prepared file, place your cursor at the position in your document where you want to insert the file.

Type: SHFT F10 (**RETRIEVE TEXT**)

Response: Document to be retrieved:

If you know the filename you want to place in your current document, enter it. If you're not sure of the filename or are unsure of which subdirectory the file is located in,

Type: F5 (**LIST FILES**)

Response: You're shown the currently active subdirectory.

If it's the correct subdirectory, press (**RETURN**). If the file you want to retrieve is in a different subdirectory, type in the name of the correct subdirectory and press (**RETURN**).

In either case, scroll through the files using your up/down and left/right cursor control keys. When you locate the file,

Select: Option 1 (**RETRIEVE**)

Response: Retrieve into current document?   (Y/N) No

Type: Y

Response: The text of the file you saved will flow into your current document. If you've selected a multi-column newsletter format with newspaper-type columns, for example, the text will be reformatted as you defined.

TIP: Remember that the text will be imported using the typeface, type size, type style and alignment it was saved in, *not* the type characteristics currently active in your file.

Reformatting a Retrieved File

You may want to reformat the retrieved file to correspond to the type characteristics of your current document. To do this, position your cursor at the point in the document where the file was retrieved.

Type: ALT F3 (**REVEAL CODES**)

Response: The screen is divided. You'll see that the contents of the retrieved file follow a description of the formatting (page layout and type specifications) of the imported file.

To reformat the retrieved file to make it conform with your current file,

Type: Use your Backspace or (**DELETE**) keys to erase the formatting commands of the retrieved file.

Response: Instantly, the file is reformatted to reflect the typeface, type size and alignment of your currently active document.

Expanded Memory and the WordPerfect Library

Although WordPerfect has powerful built-in desktop publishing features, it also can be used in conjunction with other software programs. Examples of this might include

a) Creating sophisticated newsletter mastheads or business logos with separate "draw" or "paint" programs to place in various kinds of boxes. Typical programs might include Windows Draw, GEM Draw and PC Paintbrush.

b) Creating graphs and charts with spreadsheet programs, such as WordPerfect's PlanPerfect, Lotus 1-2-3 or SuperCalc 4.

c) Importing scanned photographs created with such programs as Aldus Snapshot.

The WordPerfect Corporation publishes a supplementary software program, the WordPerfect Library, which makes it easy to locate and place files created with other software programs. It's an excellent supplement to WordPerfect for several reasons.

On the most elementary level, the WordPerfect Library is valuable because it lets you access WordPerfect, or any other software program, by pressing a single letter that corresponds to the program you want to load. Instead of facing a blank screen with a naked **C:\>** prompt, for example, you're shown a list of up to twenty programs available on your hard disk.

When you press the letter corresponding to the program you want to use, the WordPerfect Library automatically selects the proper subdirectory in which the program has been saved and loads the program.

The WordPerfect Library is further enhanced when used with expanded memory boards, such as the Intel AboveBoard. By using them together, you temporarily can leave the Word-Perfect document you're working on, load and operate another software program and, when you're finished, immediately return to the exact cursor position where you left your original WordPerfect document.

The WordPerfect Library, in other words, lets you "swap" programs between your computer's working memory and a special memory storage area. The WordPerfect Library and an expanded memory board let you work around the normal 640K limitation of the Microsoft MS-DOS operating system.

Returning to MS-DOS

Another reason you'll appreciate the WordPerfect Library and an expanded memory board is that you temporarily can leave the WordPerfect document you're working on—without closing the file—and exit to DOS, so that you can format a new diskette or create a subdirectory for a new project.

To use this feature,

Type: CTRL F1 (**SHELL**)

Response: 1 Go to DOS: 0

Type: 1

Return to the **ROOT** directory, if you aren't already there.

You'll now be able to execute any MS-DOS command. When you're finished and want to return to your place in the WordPerfect document,

Type: EXIT (Note that you must spell it out. The **EXIT** command (F7) doesn't work.)

Type: (RETURN)

You'll be returned to the exact cursor position in the Word-Perfect document you were editing when you executed **SHELL** (CTRL F1).

Using WordPerfect with Other Programs

To temporarily leave WordPerfect and enter another program,

Type: ALT SHFT and the letter that corresponds to the new software program you want to enter.

Response: WordPerfect and the document you've been working on are placed in expanded memory, and the new program is loaded.

When you've finished working with the program, exit it in the normal way. You'll then be returned to the Library Shell program.

Type: A (the letter normally assigned to WordPerfect in the Word-Perfect Library.)

Response: The WordPerfect program and the document(s) you've been working on will be returned to active status.

TIP: If the second program is a WordPerfect program, such as the PlanPerfect spreadsheet or DataPerfect database management system, you can go directly from the program back to WordPerfect.

Type: ALT SHFT and A (assuming A is the letter referring to Word-Perfect).

This bypasses the Shell and directly returns you to your WordPerfect document.

Other Library Features

In addition to letting you swap WordPerfect with other programs, the WordPerfect Library contains a powerful calculator and a versatile calendar that you easily can enter and leave.

The latest version of the WordPerfect Library, Version 2.0, also has a time management module that lets you keep track of time spent working with various software programs or on specific projects. Consultants and writers will appreciate these enhancements at billing time! Version 2.0 of the WordPerfect Library also includes a telephone dialing utility, useful for modem-users.

Working with the Clipboard

The latest version of the WordPerfect Library, Version 2.0, has a Clipboard feature that lets you easily exchange text or graphics from one software program to another without storing and retrieving complete files.

For example, let's say you're working on a WordPerfect document and want to insert drop-caps for the first letter of the first word of each major section of your document.

Type: SHFT ALT H

H is based on the assumption that your favorite draw or paint program is accessed through this letter of the WordPerfect Library Shell.

Using the drawing program, create an alphabet of special characters to be used as drop-caps.

Highlight, or outline, the letter you've created, and copy it to the Library's Clipboard.

Exit the drawing program and re-enter WordPerfect.

Position the cursor in the **CHARACTER BOX** you've created at the beginning of the first paragraph in the new section of your document.

Type: CTRL F1 (**SHELL**)

Select: Option 2 (**CLIPBOARD**)

Select: Option 4 (**RETRIEVE A GRAPHICS FILE**)

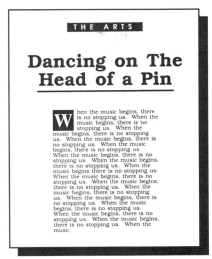

In a similar way, you can add graphs and charts created with PlanPerfect to proposals and reports you're creating with WordPerfect. The Clipboard feature also allows you to import segments of a PlanPerfect spreadsheet into a formal proposal or presentation.

More WordPerfect Library Uses

If you created a graphics file but forgot its filename, the WordPerfect Library makes it easy to enter the draw or paint-type file quickly to use the program's particular "open file" command to see which files have been created.

Or you can leave WordPerfect temporarily and enter DOS, select the subdirectory in which you may have stored the file, and use the MS-DOS **DIR** command to scan the subdirectory.

You'll quickly grow to appreciate the flexibility the Library adds to WordPerfect's basic word processing and desktop publishing capabilities. By using the library, you can consolidate several programs into good-looking, effective print communications.

Moving On

This concludes Section One of *Desktop Publishing with Word-Perfect*. You now have learned what WordPerfect 5.0 can do. However, knowing the basic commands and functions is just part of the overall picture.

Section Two completes the picture by focusing on the design considerations involved in creating newsletters, brochures, advertisements and other documents.

The section begins with a discussion of the importance of planning your documents—making accurate, actual-size layouts you can use to set up margins and column widths. You also can plan the size and placement of the various types of boxes used in your desktop publishing activities.

SECTION TWO

DESIGN TIPS AND TRICKS

10
Planning and Producing Documents

Desktop publishing with WordPerfect differs from desktop publishing with dedicated page layout programs in several important ways. To use WordPerfect successfully, a thorough understanding of these differences is crucial. Although you can create publications that are virtually indistinguishable from those created with page layout programs, you have to be comfortable working in a different way.

Because it doesn't have an on-screen grid, WordPerfect demands more planning than do dedicated page layout programs. A grid is a background of horizontal and vertical dashed lines that helps define the location of the various elements (borders, headlines and columns, etc.). Most grids have a "magnetic attraction," which helps align text and graphic elements precisely.

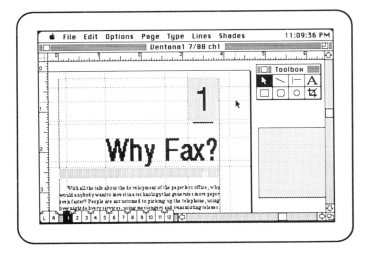

In addition, the WordPerfect screen doesn't include the horizontal and vertical rulers found on page layout programs.

You can compensate for the lack of a background grid and on-screen rulers in two ways:

a) Your initial layouts should be planned more precisely. Place headlines, columns of text and graphics boxes mathematically instead of empirically "grabbing" and placing them.

b) Train yourself to pay attention to the location of the cursor, as indicated in the lower right-hand corner of the screen. It's important to know the "longitude" and "latitude" of the cursor because, in many cases, you're not able to see all the elements on a page until you **VIEW DOCUMENT** (SHFT F7, 6) or **PRINT** (SHFT F7, 2).

All this can work to your advantage, as increased planning often results in a more cohesive design than the sometimes "free-form" designs generated from dedicated page layout programs.

You also must learn to handle text differently. Unless you've chosen a big-screen monitor or the Hercules RamFont graphics card (described in Appendix A), you won't see accurate on-screen representations of different typefaces, type sizes or type styles as you work (e.g., 36-point Helvetica bold headlines appear to be the same size as 11-point Times Roman body copy on the screen).

Again, you can use WordPerfect's **STYLE** command (ALT F8) to turn this into an advantage. Often, documents produced with page layout programs include too many typefaces, sizes and styles. By carefully limiting your type choices and storing them as **STYLE**s, you can increase page-to-page consistency and improve the appearance of your publications.

As a result of training yourself to plan and measure, you'll produce attractive, easy-to-read publications that will reflect well upon you and your company. In addition, you'll be able to take advantage of such features as WordPerfect's extensive document-organizing tools and spell-checker feature that will give your project thoroughness and professionalism.

Planning Your Project

Planning your desktop publishing projects can be divided into four distinct stages. The first two require conventional graphic design materials: tissue paper, soft pencils and plenty of erasers. The last two stages are executed on your computer using WordPerfect.

The first stage involves creating "thumbnail sketches" (reduced-size rough layouts) that convey the overall effect you want to achieve.

Translating those rough layouts into accurate, actual-size drawings is the second stage.

The third stage involves translating the dimensions and type specifications of your sketched layouts into electronic page layouts. In many cases, you'll use WordPerfect's extensive macro and stylesheet capabilities to do that.

The fourth and final step is to produce your document and add the refinements that make the document's design quality leap from "adequate" to "outstanding." Changes undoubtedly will suggest themselves as your project evolves. Some changes will become obvious as you preview your project, using WordPerfect's **VIEW DOCUMENT** command (SHFT F7, 6). Other changes only will become obvious when you either **PRINT** individual pages (SHFT F7, 2) or your entire project (SHFT F7, 1). In either case, WordPerfect's **REVEAL CODES** command (ALT F3) makes it easy to incorporate last-minute design changes.

As you refine your design, you'll probably find that being able to edit previously created macros and **STYLE**s greatly simplifies the process of making formatting changes.

Let's review these stages in greater detail.

Developing Thumbnail Sketches

This step could be called "The Cocktail Napkin School of Design." Its purpose is to establish a rough idea of how you want your finished project to look.

Because this layout is for your eyes only, you can work as quickly and roughly as you want. Use heavy curly lines to indicate headlines, thin parallel lines to show captions and body copy, and boxes to indicate where you'll insert charts, graphs, drawings or photographs.

At this stage of the game, previously published ads, brochures or newsletters can offer a wealth of ideas and solutions to design problems. To get your creative juices flowing, you might consider skimming through such publications as *The New Yorker, Communications Arts, Print* or your daily newspaper. During this "inspiration" phase, you might want to pay special attention to your industry's trade journals and magazines. Or you might leaf through books, such as the annual *The One Show* (which highlights the nation's best advertising and brochures).

TIP: Many graphic artists maintain "swipe files," more politely termed "idea files." Devote a drawer in your file cabinet to examples of "good" and "bad" design. Add to it every time you find a document containing elements you like or dislike.

Use hanging file folders to divide the drawer into ads, brochures and newsletters. Use 3M Post-it notes attached to each project to jot down the reasons you chose each piece (e.g., "good border treatment," "masthead overwhelms page and fights with headline," etc.). By referring to your file whenever you start a new project, you'll find your ideas begin to flow more quickly.

The goal of an idea file isn't to copy the work of others, but to learn from and be inspired by it. It's important to note that as you plan and produce a document, it inevitably will change, taking on a life of its own. By the time you've finished, your project probably will bear little resemblance to its original "inspiration."

Generating Accurate Layouts

After you've created a satisfying reduced-size thumbnail sketch of your project, translate it to full-size sample pages. Work as accurately as possible, using a ruler and triangle to create accurate vertical lines. Be particularly careful to establish accurate

- Top, bottom and side margins
- Border size and placement
- Number and location of columns

- Placement of headers and footers
- Occurrences of white space, such as "sinks" (extra white space at the top of each page or some pages)

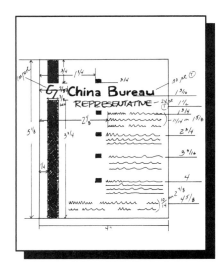

Chances are, you'll create more than one page setup for each project. For example, if you're working on a newsletter, you'll probably create separate page layouts for

- Front page (with your masthead and firm's logo)
- Inside pages
- Back page

If you're producing a book, you'll probably establish separate page layouts for

- Table of contents page
- Lists of figures, graphs and drawings
- Introduction
- The first page of each chapter
- Typical chapter left- and right-hand pages
- Bibliography and index

Save those drawings for future reference.

Creating Electronic Page Layouts

The third step is to translate the dimensions of your final layouts into macros and **STYLE**s for each project. For example, you might want to create your layout in the following sequence:

- Accurately measure the top, bottom and side margins of your layout, open a new document and create a macro that establishes the appropriate page layout.

- Measure the column widths you established on your page layout, as well as the placement of each column and the distance between them. Create a macro that establishes these column specifications.

- Measure the size and placement of page borders, and create a macro that places these borders on each page.

- Likewise, if necessary, create macros for placing vertical lines between columns on each page.

- Select the typefaces, sizes and styles to be used in your document. Create a macro that quickly chooses the **BASE FONT** for your project. Then, create **STYLE**s for each time you change type characteristics. For example, **STYLE**s can be used for headlines or chapter headings, primary subheads, secondary subheads, body copy, captions and footnotes.

- Develop macros for creating and placing any necessary **FIGURE, TABLE, TEXT** or **USER-DEFINED BOX**es. For example, if you're going to include a **USER-DEFINED BOX** for placing your logo on each page, create a macro that quickly adds the box to each page.

TIP: At this point, you might want to review the information in Chapter Eight showing how **STYLE**s created for one document can be shared by other documents.

After you've created macros to define basic page layout specifications for the various aspects of each page, create chained macros—macros that contain other macros—that quickly set up more than one specification simultaneously.

For example, if you're producing a monthly newsletter, create a **NEWSPG1** macro that sets up the front page of your newsletter, complete with a **USER-DEFINED** masthead box. Then, create **NEWSPGLF** and **NEWSPGRT** macros for setting up the inside pages. Finally, create a **NEWSBACK** macro for the back page of your newsletter, complete with address panel. Each of these macros will contain individual macros for establishing margins, borders, columns and vertical rules.

Producing and Refining Your Document

Creating separate macros, and chaining them together as described above, simplifies the process of making changes as your work proceeds. By using separate macros for margins, columns, boxes and type selection, you easily can change one or all of those elements as you work.

For example, if you want to change several pages throughout your document, you only have to edit the specific macro involved, instead of changing the column setup specifications on the three separate macros used to define your newsletter's inside pages.

It's important to understand that you'll rarely achieve perfection on your first attempt. Excellence can be achieved only to the extent that you frequently use WordPerfect's **VIEW DOCUMENT** (SHFT F7, 6) and **PRINT** (SHFT F7, 2) commands and revise your work as you move along. You'll undoubtedly find yourself changing the location and size of such design elements as borders, headlines and text columns.

As you become more comfortable with electronic publishing, you'll become more sensitive to the major impact that slight changes in line placement or line thicknesses can have.

Templates and Libraries

Templates are formatted, blank documents that contain macros and **STYLE**s for creating all the necessary page layout elements—headers, footers, column layouts, boxes and type specifications. Created by saving files composed of "empty" page layouts, templates don't contain words or graphics, just the formatted framework in which text and graphics are placed.

Templates also can be developed from previously created documents. For example, you can assemble the March issue of your newsletter using the basic elements of the January issue. You simply change the specific text and illustrations of the earlier issue and save the new version using a different filename, which should be done immediately after opening your template file.

Type: F10 (**SAVE**)

Response: Filename of original template (e.g., **NEWSTEMP**)

Type: New filename (e.g., **MARNEWS**)

Type: (RETURN)

TIP: To avoid destroying your original files accidentally, you can store all of your project templates in a separate subdirectory. For further data integrity, you can back up templates on floppy diskettes, stored in a separate location.

Six Steps to Success

It's impossible to cover the subject of graphic design in a single chapter. Nevertheless, a six-step sequence can help you design and produce better-looking, easier-to-read documents.[1]

The following steps can provide a perspective on the sequence of events and some design decisions involved in transforming your pencil and paper layouts into more elaborate electronic page layouts with WordPerfect.

---

[1]For a fuller description of the principles of graphic design, see *Looking Good in Print*, listed in the appendix.

TIP: As the following sequence shows, when designing your projects, you'll usually find it helpful to start from the page borders and work toward the inside.

Step One: Setting Margins

Start by establishing the page margins. To establish left and right margins,

Type: SHFT F8 (**FORMAT**)

Select: Option 1 (**LINE**)

Select: Option 7 (**MARGINS**)

Response: The cursor advances to the one-inch, left-hand default, which you can change to the dimension you want.

Type: (RETURN) (if you wish to accept the default; or type in a new number, followed by (**RETURN**).)

Response: This advances you to the right-hand default.

To establish top and bottom margins,

Type: SHFT F8 (**FORMAT**)

Select: Option 2 (**PAGE**)

Select: Option 5 (**MARGINS—TOP, BOTTOM**)

Response: The cursor appears, blinking under the one-inch default measure for the top margin.

Type: (RETURN) (to accept the default, or type in a new number, followed by (**RETURN**).)

TIP: The location of these margins usually will be determined by the borders you create. Remember that the more white space surrounding your publication, the more "open" and readable it will appear. Margins that are too close to the edge of a page "darken" the page. Borders and white space surrounding a document frame and isolate it from its surroundings.

Compare this...   with this...

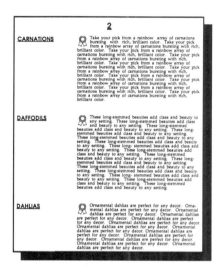
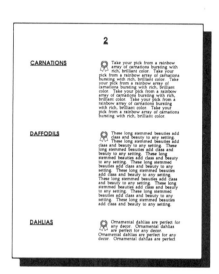

Step Two: Creating Borders

Next, using WordPerfect's **GRAPHICS** command (ALT F9), create rules and boxes that will frame your project and force the reader's eyes into the publication. (Refer to Chapter Two, if necessary, to review the steps involved in creating rules and boxes.)

TIP: If you're going to include headers and footers on each page, be sure to compensate for them by adjusting the vertical placement of the rules and boxes defining your page margins. For example, if you want your headers to appear above the top border of each page, lower the rule or box used to create the top border. If you want footers to appear below the bottom border, raise the rule or box.

Compare this...   with this...

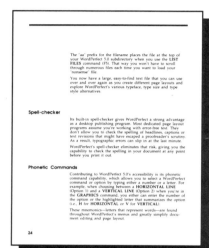
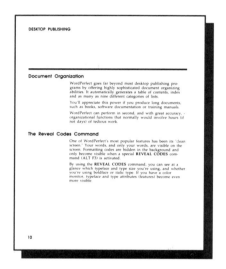

Then establish the placement of text on each page. Use WordPerfect's **MATH/COLUMNS** command (ALT F7, 4) to establish column position, column width and the distance between columns.   (Review Chapter Three for more details.)

TIP: Remember to indent your left- and right-hand column margins so that type doesn't overlap or appear too close to your page borders. Pay particular attention to the spacing between columns.

Compare this...   with this...

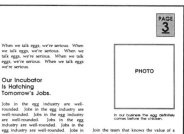

Remember to use blank **USER-DEFINED BOX**es (see Chapter Two), to "force" white space at the top and bottom of each page, between top and bottom page borders, and the beginning and end of each column of type.

Compare this...   with this...

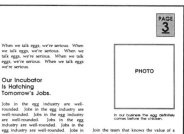

273

If you're formatting a book, for example, you can use blank **USER-DEFINED BOX**es to create extra white space to emphasize the first pages of each chapter.

Step Three: Typography

Use WordPerfect's **FONT** (CTRL F8) and **STYLE** (ALT F8) commands to choose the typefaces, type sizes and type styles for your document. Also, use the **FORMAT** command (SHFT F8) to adjust line spacing and tab settings, and to choose between flush-left/ragged-right and justified type. You might want to refer to Chapter Six to review the basic commands used in setting type with WordPerfect.

As described in Chapter Eight, WordPerfect's **STYLE**s help you save time and achieve consistency as you change type attributes for headlines, subheads, body copy and captions.

When establishing **STYLE**s, decide how you want type placed in columns. Justified type, in which the right- and left-hand edges of each column are aligned, is often chosen for "formal" documents. It increases word density—the number of words that fit in a given space.

For a more informal, "contemporary" document, flush-left/ragged-right type gives an "open" feeling, because of the irregular amounts of white space that appear at the end of each line.

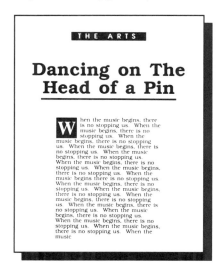

In deciding whether to use WordPerfect's **HYPHENATION** feature, remember that even flush-left/ragged-right columns can benefit from hyphenation. It can help prevent unnaturally large gaps of white space at the end of lines.

> We observed the brownish fox jumping happily around the sleeping puppy. We observed the brownish fox jumping happily around the sleeping puppy. We observed the brownish fox jumping happily around the sleeping puppy. We observed the brownish fox jumping happily around the sleeping puppy. We observed the brownish fox

Hyphenated justified type increases word density and cuts down on the amount of white space between words. However, hyphenation used in narrow columns with large type often results in too many hyphenated words, making columns difficult to read. As a rule of thumb, avoid having more than three hyphenated lines in a row.

> Remember to always be courteous, attentive, responsive and know-ledgeable about your pro-duct. Remember to al-ways be courteous, atten-tive, responsive, and

As a final typographic refinement, use WordPerfect's **TAB SET** command (ALT F8, 1, 8) to adjust the depth of indention. Remember that the standard half-inch tab setting that looks good on a typed manuscript often looks exaggerated when text is typeset in a multi-column format. This is particularly true as type size decreases.

An interesting correlation exists between column width and type size. Large type in narrow columns often is difficult to read.

16-point text placed on a 12 pica column is also very difficult to read.

Similarly, small type in wide columns can be difficult to read. The reader's eyes have to make too many "jumps" and can become "lost" when moving from the right-hand end of one line to the beginning of the next line.

7-point text placed on a 24-pica column is very difficult to read. 7-point text placed on a 24-pica column is very difficult to read. 7-point text placed on a 24-pica column is very difficult to read. 7-point text placed on a 24-pica column is very difficult to read. 7-point text placed on a 24-pica column is very difficult to read. 7-point text placed on a 24-pica column is very difficult to read. 7-point text placed on a 24-pica column is very difficult to read. 7-point text placed on a 24-pica column is very difficult to read. 7-point text placed on a

Line spacing, or leading, also should enter the equation. Narrow columns with small type often work best with WordPerfect's automatic line spacing. But, as line lengths become longer, extra space should be added between the lines of type.

Compare this...

Typography is a craft that requires careful attention to detail. Typography is a craft that requires careful attention to detail. Typography is a craft that requires careful attention to detail.

with this...

Typography is a craft that requires careful attention to detail. Typography is a craft that requires careful attention to detail. Typography is a craft that requires careful attention to detail. Typography is a craft that requires careful attention to detail. Typography is a

As a rule of thumb, small type works best in narrow columns with normal, or tight, line spacing. As columns become wider, larger type and extra leading look best.

This relationship depends upon the particular typeface you choose, because each typeface has its own horizontal length and colors the page in a different way. In the example below, note how different typefaces set in the same size have vastly different word density levels.

**The quick brown fox
jumped over the lazy dog.**

**The quick brown fox
jumped over the lazy dog.**

**The quick brown fox
jumped over the lazy dog.**

*The quick brown fox
jumped over the lazy dog.*

Spacing between Columns

Space between columns should be correctly proportioned to column width. Large type set in wide columns requires more space between columns than small type set in narrow columns.

Compare this...   with this...

Step Four: Graphic Accents

The next step is to create macros for the various sizes of rules and boxes you're likely to need throughout your document. For example, if you're working on a multi-column newsletter and are using horizontal bars to separate adjacent articles, create a macro that quickly creates the bar each time you need it. (See Chapter Three for a review.)

Remember to use WordPerfect's **GRAPHICS** command (ALT F9) to create the type of **TEXT**, **TABLE**, **FIGURE** or **USER-DEFINED BOX** you want in your documents. You might want to review the techniques described in Chapter Five regarding the modification of border style, caption placement and positioning, background shading, as well as the spacing of text inside and around the boxes.

Step Five: Document Organization

Next, add organizing elements, such as page numbers, headers and footers. These commands are grouped under WordPerfect's **FORMAT** command (SHFT F8). Remember that header and footer information, including page numbers, usually differs on left- and right-hand pages.

Step Six: Final Touches

If you're preparing a long document, such as a book or training manual, review the sections of Chapter Four that describe how WordPerfect automatically generates an index, table of contents, automatic references, lists of figures, tables, drawings and photographs, as well as endnotes and footnotes. You can save a lot of last-minute writing and editing by including the proper commands in your document as you write it.

TIP: As you go through the six-step process outlined above, use WordPerfect's **MACRO** and **STYLE** features to store your project specifications. As described in earlier chapters, you easily can modify them as you go along.

Moving On

The following chapters provide detailed descriptions and illustrations of some types of desktop publishing projects you're likely to design and produce with WordPerfect 5.0.

11

WordPerfect in Action

When you've learned to use WordPerfect's graphics features, you'll find that the appearance of nearly any document can be enhanced. In this chapter, you'll examine a potpourri of documents that can be created with WordPerfect 5.0, and you'll learn valuable design techniques and shortcuts.

These documents shouldn't be interpreted as rigid prototypes of appropriate design; rather use them to glean ideas on making your project more effective.

Remember that experimentation and "creative dissatisfaction" are stepping stones that lead to good design. An element from an advertisement might work well in your newsletter, just as a stylesheet for a training manual might suit your in-house tabloid.

Let's briefly examine some of the ways you're likely to use WordPerfect's graphics features. The following examples contain design tips and suggestions. However, you'll undoubtedly add your own expertise to refine the design of these documents.

Business Correspondence

All types of business correspondence—letterheads, proposals, invoices, forms, memos and reports—can be made more readable, persuasive and enjoyable by using simple desktop publishing techniques.

You can produce attractive stationery and envelopes with WordPerfect, particularly if you import images using other graphics software. Remember that your company identity is all-important. If necessary, use the services of a graphic artist to design lasting professional images.

You also can create forms, reports and other documents that require constant updating. Strive to attain an overall company image by incorporating similar visual features in all your documents, particularly those that will be seen outside the company.

Advertisements

If you regularly run sales-oriented advertising in daily or weekly publications, you'll find that desktop publishing offers you a way to quickly update specifics and still retain the overall format of the ad. This can save many hundreds of dollars in traditional typesetting and paste-up costs. And it's easier to meet deadlines on last-minute sales and other time-sensitive advertising.

Remember that desktop publishing can't do everything yet. If your ads include photographs or illustrations, don't try to scan them in or import them. Instead, create a bordered box that indicates the size of your graphic. Then give your sales representative instructions on how to drop it into your ad. (Most magazines and newspapers will strip in artwork for a small fee.) Your all-important graphic images will be sharper and more appealing.

Newsletters

The timeliness and relative simplicity of newsletters make them a natural for WordPerfect's new desktop publishing features. Stylesheets and macros can speed your work, particularly for longer newsletters with high page-to-page consistency.

If your masthead is more complicated than WordPerfect can handle, have it produced by other means, and your printer can drop it into your camera-ready art. You can create a blank user-defined box to indicate position.

Consider having a graphic artist help you with the masthead and overall design of your newsletter—it's a worthwhile, one-time cost.

Always save old newsletters—the copy, as well as the macros and stylesheets. You'll be surprised how many times you'll use repeating elements, such as lists of sales offices, revised products or annual events.

Catalogs

Because catalogs require constant revisions and often are formatted rigidly, you'll find WordPerfect to be a prolific production tool.

First, decide which pages you want to produce with WordPerfect and which are better suited for production by other methods. For example, catalog covers are often multicolored, with elaborate graphics and unusual type treatments—inappropriate for WordPerfect at this time.

If your catalog is to be produced on glossy ("slick") paper, consider outputting your work on a Linotronic or a similar machine that produces typeset-quality material.

Training Manuals, Books and Longer Documents

Although long, unwieldy documents, such as user manuals, pamphlets and books, can be created successfully, your work will be speeded greatly if you use WordPerfect macros and stylesheets for repetitive, complex page layouts.

For large projects, you may want to contract a designer to plan the overall appearance, then use WordPerfect to produce the final product. A designer is a one-time expense that will more than return your investment, particularly if you're planning large print runs or multiple printings.

Moving On

As you'll see in the following pages, WordPerfect can create or duplicate hundreds of different kinds of documents—resumes, warranty cards, menus, invoices, purchase orders, spec sheets, announcements, invitations and more. The following examples show only a few of the many effects that can be achieved.

The importance of developing accurate sketches before executing your design can't be over-emphasized. Future versions of WordPerfect probably will allow you to edit graphics features directly on your screen. Until then, avoid bouncing back and forth between text and **VIEW DOCU-MENT**. The more thoroughly you develop your design beforehand, the more successful you'll be in creating your documents.

As with any new technology, you must balance the time spent obtaining a result with the time saved having it done the "old way." The solution often lies somewhere in the middle, and you'll probably find yourself using a combination of desktop publishing and traditional cut-and-paste techniques to get the job done quickly and inexpensively.

Keep experimenting, and always be on the lookout for new graphics ideas. Your design skills will grow as WordPerfect desktop publishing features become more versatile and powerful with each new version.

Advertisements

Display Classified Advertising

Newspapers often allow you to furnish camera-ready artwork, which puts you in control of copy and design. You can create eye-catching borders, headlines and typefaces for smaller classifieds that will make them stand out among competing advertisements.

The screens were created using two separate figure boxes.

When boxes touch each other, be sure to specify any matching border styles you might want. In this example, the top screen had **0** border for the bottom, right and left, but **single** for the top. Otherwise, a borderless screen would have hurt continuity.

Bullets were dropped in using WordPerfect's character sets. Check your printer to see which sets it recognizes.

ꓥREPRESENTATIVE
for our China Bureau

■ Exciting career opportunity for talented, outgoing individual. Must be experienced travel representative.

■ Position includes 20% travel to various cities in China. Must have flexible schedule.

■ Generous benefit program including paid vacations, sick leave, insurance plan, and other benefits.

■ Applications being accepted immediately. Apply in person at the Global Travel office at 100 Side Street, Los Angeles, CA 00010.

Global Travel is an equal opportunity employer and does not discriminate on the basis of race, religion, sex, handicap, or non-specific jet lag afflictions.

Display Classified Advertising

Remember that graphics boxes must be created and positioned separately. You can't create a box within a box or manipulate graphics within a box. Additional boxes must be layered over the master figure box and "jockeyed" into position, often using trial-and-error methods.

If you develop a sketch before producing the ad, you'll have a better idea of how many boxes you need, as well as your required measurements.

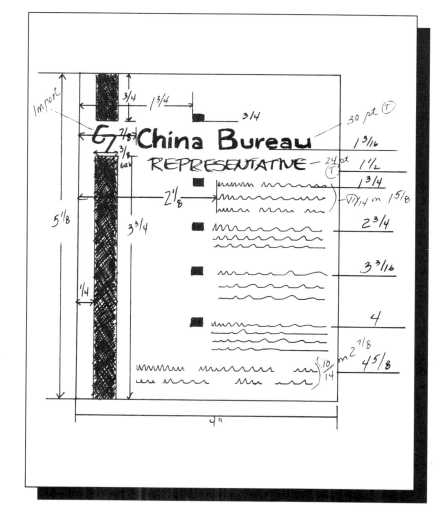

Flyers

This example shows how the simple juxtaposition of boxes and thick rules can create sophisticated effects.

First, create three boxes. Then position lines around them, either by using a ruler or by noting horizontal positions of the boxes.

Four separate vertical lines were created, uniformly spaced from borders of boxes.

Often it's easier to print out unfinished work, then measure the remaining elements, rather than to try to position graphics on-screen.

Flyers

Don't be discouraged if you initially fail to produce the effect you want with more complex visuals. Remember, all graphic design is a series of trial-and-error steps. Often you must rely on a combination of intuition and well-established rules.

Note how different type sizes and weights emphasize **SummerFair** and the date.

The **S** and **F** are different sized fonts (rather than an upper- and lower-case font) creating a more uniform, stylized headline.

Remember to maintain uniform distances between rules and boxes, and always check with a ruler to make certain they're aligned on the final print-out.

Note that boxes are transparent and don't cover up overlapping lines or screens when placed over other boxes.

DOGPATCH

SummerFair

Sponsored by the Dogpatch County Town Bureau

AT ROLLING RIVER

JULY 9-10

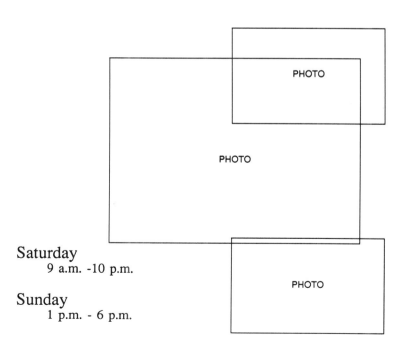

PHOTO

PHOTO

Saturday
9 a.m. -10 p.m.

Sunday
1 p.m. - 6 p.m.

PHOTO

Business Correspondence

Letterheads

Keep stationery design simple and uncluttered, with a clearly defined writing area. Envelopes should reflect the same elements and style as your letterhead.

Clip art was imported from WordPerfect's graphics files.

Early 5.0 users may find that WordPerfect produces lines of varying thicknesses even though lines of equal thickness were specified.

You can't specify a position when creating white space. Instead, use hard returns to space down to the address line, then place the cursor on the next horizontal line.

The Seafood Barn

1001 Main Street SE,   Miami, Ohio 48900   (919) 922-2222

Business Cards

If you have a number of employees, you can group business cards on the same page and change names and addresses when appropriate. This saves time and cuts preparation and printing costs.

You'll save time if you know your vertical and horizontal positions before importing graphics.

Either all or none of the image area can be screened. Because the graphic was imported with a figure box, attempting to screen only the logo would create undesirable results.

The logo was imported from a WordPerfect graphics file using a figure box with the **none** border option.

You may need to play around with size and position until you get the desired result.

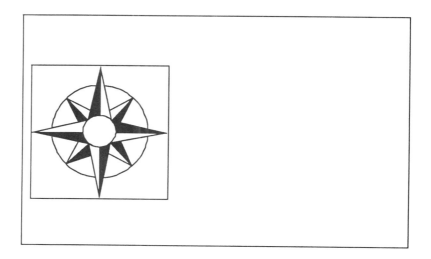

Reports and Proposals

Typewritten reports and proposals are dull, although they often need to be persuasive and quickly read.

PROPOSAL

INVESTMENT OPPORTUNITIES
FOR THE FREQUENT TRAVELER

To:

Board of Directors

Stock Holders

New Investors

Loan Sharks

September 19, 1988

Reports and Poposals

One of the most attractive aspects of using WordPerfect for desktop publishing is that simple graphic elements can be added while the document is being produced with little or no extra time and effort expended.

Use thick horizontal lines, screened at 20 percent, to create interesting borders, headers and footers.

Experiment with letter spacing to provide breathing room for short headlines with big type.

Work with horizontal lines creatively to provide "quick and dirty" graphic design.

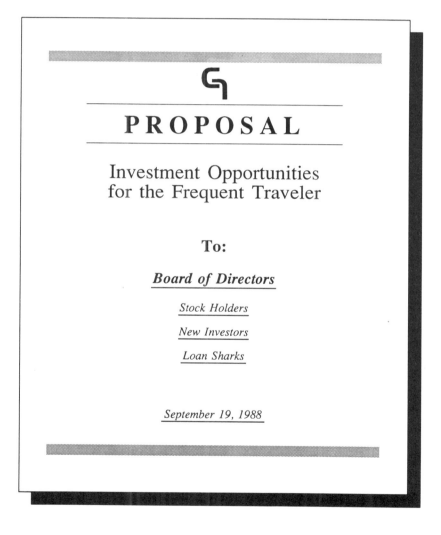

Reports and Proposals

These examples show two ways you can make documents more readable by manipulating graphic elements.

A photo or illustration placed within the text area helps break up monotonous type.

Headlines placed in margins allow readers to obtain critical information at a glance.

PROPOSAL

Travel Rates Increasing

Even though travel rates are increasing, travelers can save more money than ever. Even though travel rates are increasing, travelers can save more money than ever. Even though travel rates are increasing, travelers can save more money than ever. Even though travel rates are increasing, travelers can save more money than ever. Even though travel rates are increasing, travelers can save more money than ever. Even though travel rates are increasing, travelers can save more money than ever. Even though travel rates are increasing, travelers can save more money than ever. Even though travel rates are increasing, travelers can save more money than ever. Even though travel rates are increasing, travelers can save more money than ever. Even though travel rates are increasing, travelers can save more money than ever.

Better Buys

Our frequent traveler plan provides a great investment opportunity. Our frequent traveler plan provides a great investment opportunity. Our frequent traveler plan provides a great investment opportunity. Our frequent traveler plan provides a great investment opportunity. Our frequent traveler plan provides a great investment opportunity. Our frequent traveler

Reports and Proposals

Although these two examples differ considerably, there's no "right" or "wrong" solution. Either is acceptable, depending upon your particular document.

Because it's cursor-controlled, you can't specify the exact vertical position of horizontal lines. Thus, if you need to position a line exactly, you must experiment with line spacing and line height to obtain exact position.

Pull-quotes create visual appeal and promote readership.

PROPOSAL

Travel Rates Increasing

Even though travel rates are increasing, travelers can save more money than ever. Even though travel rates are increasing, travelers can save more money than ever. Even though travel rates are increasing, travelers can save more money than ever. Even though travel rates are increasing, travelers can save more money than ever. Even though travel rates are increasing, travelers can save more money than ever. Even though travel rates are increasing, travelers can save more money than ever. Even though travel rates are increasing, travelers can save more money than ever. Even though travel rates are increasing, travelers can save more money than ever. Even though travel rates are increasing, travelers can save more money than ever.

Save money with early purchases.

Better Buys

Our frequent traveler plan provides a great investment opportunity. Our frequent traveler plan provides a great investment opportunity. Our frequent traveler plan provides a great investment opportunity. Our frequent traveler plan provides a great investment opportunity. Our frequent traveler plan provides a great investment opportunity for you.

Newsletters

WordPerfect is capable of producing any number of mastheads and formats, depending upon your tastes. Experiment with column widths and the number of columns, and the position of the contents box, headlines and subheads.

Note that the masthead screen is borderless. Outside rules would have fought with internal horizontal lines. Yet the contents are framed in a box to clearly set them off from the text.

If you want headlines to extend more than one column, create a box with wrap-around text. That will help you align columns more easily when placing text.

The top rule above the headline was created by making a box and specifying a thick border at the top, with no border on the remaining sides.

Trips 'n Things

July 1988   Monthly Newsletter for Global Travel   Vol 5

JetAir Offers Weekend Getaways to Lebano

You can now fly direct from Raleigh You can now fly direct from Raleigh You can now fly direct from Raleigh You can now fly direct from Raleigh You can now fly direct from Raleigh You can now fly direct from Raleigh You can now fly direct from Raleigh You can now fly direct from Raleigh You can now fly direct from Raleigh You can now fly direct from Raleigh You can now fly direct from Raleigh You can now fly direct from Raleigh You can now fly direct from Raleigh You can now fly direct from Raleigh You can now fly direct from Raleigh You can now fly direct from Raleigh

You can now fly direct from Raleigh You can now fly direct from Raleigh You can now fly direct from Raleigh You can now fly direct from Raleigh You can now fly direct from Raleigh You can now fly direct from Raleigh You can now fly direct from

Raleigh You can now fly direct from Raleigh You can now fly direct from Raleigh You can now fly direct from Raleigh You can now fly direct from Raleigh You can now fly direct from Raleigh You can now fly direct from Raleigh You can now fly direct from Raleigh You can now fly direct from Raleigh You can now fly direct from Raleigh You can now fly direct from Raleigh You can now fly direct from Raleigh You can now fly direct from Raleigh You can now fly direct from Raleigh You can now fly direct from Raleigh You can now fly direct from Raleigh You can now fly direct from Raleigh You can now fly direct from Raleigh You can now fly direct from Raleigh You can now fly direct from Raleigh You can now fly direct from

Raleigh You can now fly direct from Raleigh You can now fly direct from Raleigh You can now fly direct from Raleigh You can now fly direct from Raleigh You can now fly direct from Raleigh You can now fly direct from Raleigh You can now fly direct from Raleigh You can now fly direct from Raleigh

Get Away

Get away from it all Get away from it all Get away from it all Get away from it all Get away from it all Get away from it all Get away from it all Get away from it all Get away from it all Get away from it all Get away from it all Get away from it all Get away from it all Get away from it all Get

continued on page 4

What's Inside

2   trips trips trips trips trips trips trips trips

3   trips trips trips trips trips trips trips trips

9   trips trips trips trips trips trips trips trips

Newsletters

Your newsletter masthead is the single most important visual element. Research other newsletters—perhaps those of your competitors—for ideas on developing or improving your masthead.

In this example, it's much easier to underline *Trips 'n Things* three times than to create horizontal lines.

Experimentation with letter spacing was required to make **Monthly Newsletter for Global Travel** fit snugly between the **p** and the **g**.

Trips 'n Things
July 1988   Monthly Newsletter for Global Travel   Vol 5

JetAir Offers Weekend Getaways to Lebano

You can now fly direct from Raleigh You can now fly direct from Raleigh You can fly direct from Raleigh fly direct from

Raleigh You can now fly direct from Raleigh You can now fly direct from Raleigh You can now fly direct from Raleigh You can now fly direct from Raleigh You can now fly direct from Raleigh You can now fly direct from Raleigh You can now fly from Raleigh y direct from fly

Raleigh You can now fly direct from Raleigh You can now fly direct from Raleigh You can now fly direct from Raleigh You can now fly direct from Raleigh You can now fly direct from Raleigh You can now fly direct from Raleigh You can now fly direct from Raleigh You can now fly direct from Raleigh

Get Away

Get away from it all Get away from it all Get away from it all Get away from it all Get away from it all Get away from it all Get away from it Get away from it all Get it all Get away m it et

Newsletters

As with any graphics project, the final result may be a hybrid of several first-draft sketches. Have a good idea of how your document will look before attempting to produce it using WordPerfect.

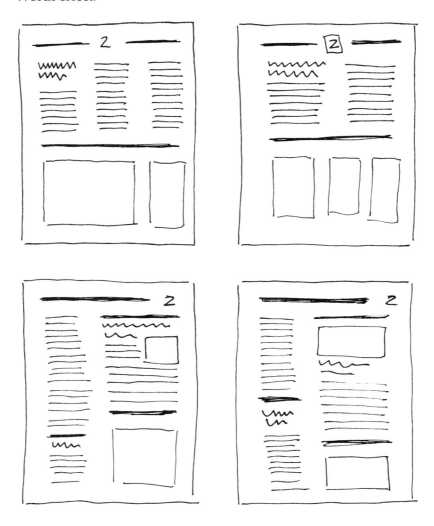

Newsletters

Graphics elements from the original cover page should carry over to inside newsletter pages. Note how the thickness and width of horizontal lines remain the same, as do screen values, type sizes and rules around boxes.

Avoid justified type in narrow columns. It can create excessive hyphenation and uneven margins.

Because you can't put horizontal lines in a user-defined box, the **UNDERLINE** command was used to create rules.

Screens call attention to important material and provide contrast on all-type pages.

2

trips trips and more exotic trips trips trips and more exotic trips trips and more exotic trips trips trips and more exotic trips trips trips and more exotic trips trips trips and more exotic trips trips trips and more exotic trips trips trips and more exotic trips trips trips and more exotic trips trips trips and more exotic trips trips and more exotic trips trips trips and more exotic trips trips trips and more exotic trips trips and more exotic trips trips trips and more exotic trips trips trips and more exotic trips trips and more exotic trips trips trips and more exotic trips trips trips and more exotic trips trips and more exotic trips trips trips and more exotic trips trips trips and more exotic trips trips and more exotic trips

Off to Maui

The beautiful road to Hana The beautiful road to Hana The beautiful road to Hana The beautiful road to Hana The beautiful road to Hana The beautiful road to Hana The beautiful road to Hana The beautiful road to Hana

See the Sunrise Over the Stunning Haleakala Crater

Walk hand in hand in the sand and watch the sun rise over the fine black sand of the Haleakala Crater Walk hand in hand in the sand and watch the sun rise over the fine black sand of the Haleakala Crater Walk hand in hand in the sand and watch the sun rise over the fine black sand of the Haleakala Crater Walk hand in hand in the sand and watch the sun rise over the fine black sand of the Haleakala Crater Walk hand in hand in the sand and watch the sun rise over the fine black sand of the Haleakala Crater

Walk hand in hand in the sand and watch the sun rise over the fine black sand of the Haleakala Crater Walk hand in hand in the sand and watch the sun rise over the fine black sand of the Haleakala Crater Walk hand in hand in the sand

PHOTO

UPCOMING EVENTS

King Kamehameha Day
June 12

London Extravaganza
June 16

Mediterranean Cruise
June 29

Catalogs

Always create accurate sketches, including measurements, *before* creating your image on-screen. Until WordPerfect is fully WYSIWYG ("What You See Is What You Get"), rough sketches prepared beforehand are preferable to playing peek-a-boo with **VIEW DOCUMENT**.

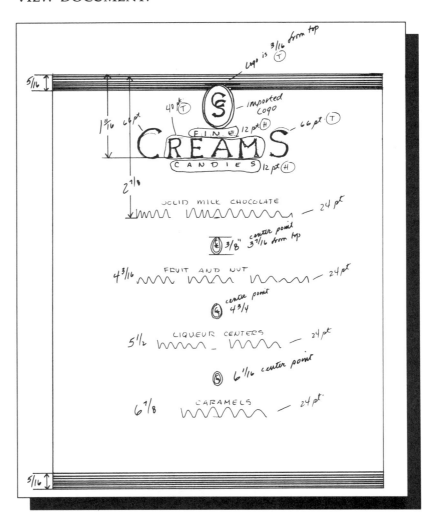

Catalogs

Creative use of type and white space often can result in simple, yet elegant catalog cover designs.

Use repeating lines of slightly different widths to produce subtly pleasing visual effects.

The **CS** logos were imported from a graphics package.

The lower "multiple line" image can be repeated by blocking and moving the appropriate codes from the image above.

FINE

CREAMS

C A N D I E S

SOLID MILK CHOCOLATE
Rich 'n' Creamy

FRUIT AND NUT
Special Filling

LIQUEUR CENTERS
Imported Flavors

CARAMELS
Chewy Delights

Catalogs

Trial-and-error experimentation with kerning, leading and font sizes will achieve a pleasing, unified image. The **REVEAL CODES** example below shows the many steps required to produce a seemingly simple all-type image.

By reducing line height, you're able to drop the word **FINE** below the ascenders **C** and **S**.

Rather than using upper- and lower-case type, specify a larger point size of the same font to create more interesting all-type effects.

```
[HRt]
[Cntr][Font:Helvetica 12 pt]F I N E[C/A/Flrt][Ln Height:0.01"][HRt]
[Cntr][Font:Times Roman 66 pt]C[Font:Times Roman 44 pt]REAM
[Font:Times Roman 66 pt]S[C/A/Flrt][Ln Height:0.9"][HRt]
[Font:Helvetica 12 pt][Cntr]C A N D I E S[C/A/Flrt][Ln Height:Auto]
[HRt]
[HRt]
```

Catalogs

In these examples, type was positioned on inside pages, then boxes were used to indicate position of photos or illustrations.

To create the top header, first type **FRUITS**, then create separate horizontal lines to the left and right.

User-defined boxes can be placed in columns just like text to automatically create even spacing between columns.

One box was created, then blocked and copied five more times.

The handy **CAPTION** feature allows you to create text that automatically attaches to specific boxes.

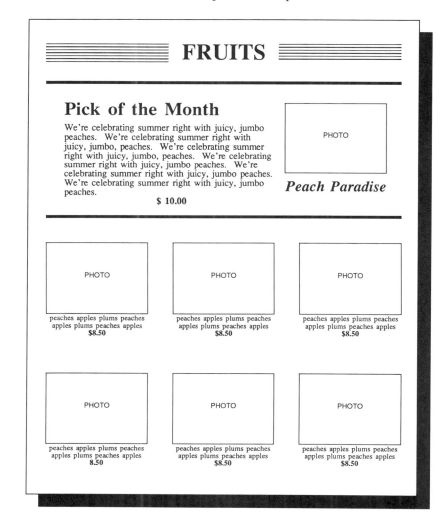

Long Documents

Covers for training manuals often appear in straight type-written format. With a little extra effort, your message can be enhanced by the creative use of fonts, screens and rules.

A borderless screen was created. Then the text was underlined to create offsetting rules.

Horizontal lines cannot be created within a box, so use the **UNDERLINE** command to create rules.

You can center text automatically left and right within a box. To center the top and bottom, use inside border space.

Experiment with letter and word spacing to align type vertically.

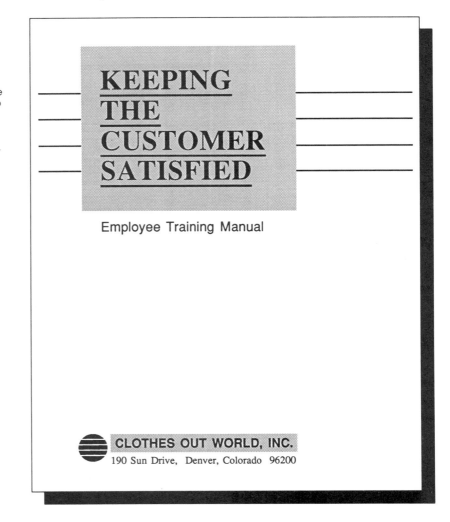

KEEPING THE CUSTOMER SATISFIED

Employee Training Manual

CLOTHES OUT WORLD, INC.
190 Sun Drive, Denver, Colorado 96200

Long Documents

Simple use of horizontal lines and screens can greatly enhance any cover sheet.

First, create the screened box and note horizontal positions of the box, left and right.

Also note vertical positions of each text line.

Then go outside the box, space down to that position and create lines to the left and right of the box, using page borders and box borders as margins.

Boxes are transparent when laid over other boxes, so horizontal lines were created separately to the left and right of the screened area.

KEEPING THE CUSTOMER SATISFIED

KEEPING THE CUSTOMER SATISFIED

Employee Training Manual

Long Documents

Note how the simple placement of six horizontal rules and two vertical rules make this document more lively and readable.

To reverse type, create a 100 percent black box, choose **color** white, then type text.

To avoid uneven column wrapping, place **COLUMN ON/OFF** at the point where you actually want text to begin.

2

The Satisfied Customer

The satisfied customer is one who is greeted with a smile, treated like a v.i.p., and leaves with exactly what he or she was looking for. The satisfied customer is one who is greeted with a smile, treated like a v.i.p., and leaves with exactly what he or she was looking for.

The satisfied customer is one who is greeted with a smile, treated like a v.i.p., and leaves with exactly what he or she was looking for. The satisfied customer is one who is greeted with a smile, treated like a v.i.p., and leaves with exactly what he or she was looking for. The satisfied customer is one who is greeted with a smile, treated like a v.i.p., and leaves with exactly what he or she was looking for. The satisfied customer is one who is greeted with a smile, treated like a v.i.p., and leaves with exactly what he or she was looking

for. The satisfied customer is one who is greeted with a smile, treated like a v.i.p., and leaves with exactly what he or she was looking for. The satisfied customer is one who is greeted with a smile, treated like a v.i.p.

Satisfied Customers Keep Coming Back

and leaves with exactly what he or she was looking for. The satisfied customer is one who is greeted with a smile, treated like a v.i.p., and leaves with exactly what he or she was looking for. The satisfied customer is one who is greeted with a smile, treated like a v.i.p., and leaves with exactly what he or she was looking for.

The satisfied customer is one who is greeted with

a smile, treated like a v.i.p., and leaves with exactly what he or she was looking for. The satisfied customer is one who is greeted with a smile, treated like a v.i.p., and leaves with exactly what he or she was looking for. The satisfied customer is one who is greeted with a smile, treated like a v.i.p., and leaves with exactly what he or she was looking for.

The satisfied customer is one who is greeted with a smile, treated like a v.i.p., and leaves with exactly what he or she was looking for. The satisfied customer is one who is greeted with a smile, treated like a v.i.p., and leaves with exactly what he or she was looking for. The satisfied customer is one who is greeted with

Long Documents

Pull-quotes are an effective way to break up long runs of text and "pull" the reader's attention into the document.

Use outside border space, instead of hard returns, to create white space above and below pull-quotes.

To force the text to wrap correctly, set up pull-quotes as boxes with borders at the top and bottom.

Then define them as a paragraph, not a page.

:ustomer
:ted with
:e a v.i.p.,
:actly
ıs looking
customer
:ted with
:e a v.i.p.,
:actly
ıs looking

:ustomer
:ted with
:e a v.i.p.,
:actly
ıs looking
customer
:ted with
:e a v.i.p.,
:actly
ıs looking
customer
:ted with
:e a v.i.p.,
:actly
ıs looking
customer
:ted with

for. The satisfied customer is one who is greeted with a smile, treated like a v.i.p., and leaves with exactly what he or she was looking for. The satisfied customer is one who is greeted with a smile, treated like a v.i.p.,

Satisfied Customers Keep Coming Back

and leaves with exactly what he or she was looking for. The satisfied customer is one who is greeted with a smile, treated like a v.i.p., and leaves with exactly what he or she was looking for. The satisfied customer is one who is greeted with a smile, treated like a v.i.p., and leaves with exactly what he or she was looking

a smile, tr
and leaves
what he o
for. The :
is one wh
a smile, tr
and leaves
what he o
for. The
is one wh
a smile, tr
and leaves
what he o
for.
    The
is one wh
a smile, tr
and leaves
what he o
for. The
is one wh
a smile, tr
and leaves

Long Documents

Watch out for "visual overkill"—too many visual elements placed on one page. Note how the reverses and screens in the body copy are repeated appropriately above with the horizontal rules and page numbers.

Note how even and odd page numbers are positioned opposite each other at the outside of the page. Stylesheets and macros can make short work of repetitive headers and footers.

Use line spacing, not hard returns, to adjust white space around the headlines.

Vertical rules between columns help frame type and visual elements within the text.

3

The satisfied customer is one who is greeted with a smile, treated like a v.i.p., and leaves with exactly what he or she was looking for. The satisfied customer is one who is greeted with a smile, treated like a v.i.p., and leaves with exactly what he or she was looking for. The satisfied customer is one who is greeted with a smile, treated like a v.i.p., and leaves with exactly what he or she was looking for.

Introducing the Product

The satisfied customer is one who is greeted with a smile, treated like a v.i.p., and leaves with exactly what he or she was looking for. The satisfied customer is one who is greeted with a smile, treated like a v.i.p., and leaves with exactly what he or she was looking for. The satisfied customer is one who is greeted with a smile, treated like a v.i.p., and leaves with exactly what he or she was looking for. The satisfied customer is one who is greeted with a smile, treated like a v.i.p., and leaves with exactly what he or she was looking for. The satisfied customer is one who is greeted with a smile, treated like a v.i.p.,

REMEMBER

COURTESY

•

PRODUCT KNOWLEDGE

•

REPROACHFUL STARES

and leaves with exactly what he or she was looking for.

The satisfied customer is one who is greeted with a smile, treated like a v.i.p., and leaves with exactly what he or she was looking for. The satisfied customer is one who is greeted with a smile, treated like a v.i.p., and leaves with exactly what he or she was looking for. The satisfied customer is one who is greeted with a smile, treated like a v.i.p., and leaves with exactly what he or she was looking for. The satisfied customer is one who is greeted with a smile, treated like a v.i.p., and leaves with exactly what he or she was looking for. The satisfied customer

is one who is greeted with a smile, treated like a v.i.p., and leaves with exactly what he or she was looking for. The satisfied customer is one who is greeted with a smile, treated like a v.i.p., and leaves with exactly what he or she was looking for. The satisfied customer is one who is greeted with a smile, treated like a v.i.p., and leaves with exactly what he or she was looking for. The satisfied customer is one who is greeted with a smile, treated like a v.i.p., and leaves with exactly what he or she was looking for. The satisfied customer is one who is greeted with a smile, treated like a v.i.p., and leaves with exactly what he or

Handling Distractions

The satisfied customer is one who is greeted with a smile, treated like a v.i.p., and leaves with exactly what he or she was looking for. The satisfied customer is one who is greeted with a smile, treated like a v.i.p., and leaves with exactly what he or she was looking for. The satisfied customer is one who is greeted with a smile, treated like a v.i.p., and leaves with exactly what he or she was looking

Long Documents

Multiple user-defined and graphics boxes can create a nearly endless variety of contrasting, yet appealing graphic images.

Always create separate boxes when using different graphics options. Here, two boxes were produced, one to create reversed type and one for a screen.

It's easier to use outside border space to create the white space between boxes than to specify that space mathematically.

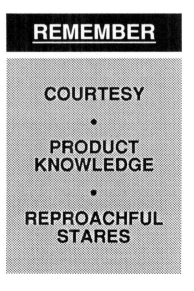

311

Other Graphics

Menus

WordPerfect allows you to import illustrations from graphics libraries and other software programs. You may want to invest in libraries of clip art and other visual enhancements.

Creative use of vertical rules creates a "barn" effect.

Use **border options** to enhance interest with borders of varying widths.

Use justified margins and dot leaders to align type with dots automatically.

Menus

Logos can be tedious to produce, and you may need design expertise to achieve satisfactory results. As this example shows, WordPerfect is capable of producing excellent logos and icons.

Type **Seafood** first to anchor your position on the page. Then position other words above and below.

Line spacing was reduced to **0.6"** from **1.0"** to allow **The** to go below ascenders **S** and **f**.

Line spacing between **Seafood** and **Barn** was changed to **.8**.

Invoices and Purchase Orders

Because you can't place lines within a box, the working section was created entirely by using horizontal and vertical lines.

Two separate boxes were used, one with a reversed screen and one with black type placed within.

If you have trouble making corners meet, just print the document and use good old white-out!

CLOTHES OUT WORLD

190 Sun Slope Drive West
Denver, Colorado 96200

INVOICE   Customer Number:

Bill to: Ship to:

Item	Quantity	Item Description	Price	Total

Subtotal	
Tax	
Total	

Thank You

Price Lists, Order Forms, Spec Sheets

Timely information can be updated almost daily, giving sales and customer service personnel instant access to important information.

Horizontal rules are used to break up type and provide easy reading.

Additional white space between rules also makes documents easier to read.

10

ITEM	PRICE	DESCRIPTION
Lawn Darts	$11.99 each set	Safety-tipped rubber lawn darts designed for easy aim and safe play. In bright colors that are easy to see. Made for beginning players yet enjoyable for all ages. Precise balanced design allows great control and accuracy in throwing for professional-style dart action.
Rubber Duckies	$4.95 each	Jumbo-sized duckies that fit the pool rather than the bathtub. Bright yellow classic design, water resistant to float, make noises when squeezed.
Beach Towels	$11.95 each	Thick, plush towels in extra-large sizes and an assortment of colorful designs such as favorite cartoon characters and movie stars.
Flip-Flops	$1.95 a pair	Assorted sizes and colors of durable, comfortable flip-flops.
T-Shirts	$5.99 each	100% cotton t-shirts in an assortment of designs and sizes.

12

Present and Future Perfect

As you've seen in the preceding chapters, WordPerfect 5.0 offers a wealth of powerful and easily accessible graphic, text and layout features.

WordPerfect 5.0 lets you design and produce attractive multi-column documents, enhanced with a wide variety of graphic accents, such as borders, rules and bars. It lets you control white space and easily integrate your words with imported graphic images, such as charts, graphs, illustrations and scanned photographs. Once placed in a WordPerfect document, these images can be easily resized, moved or distorted until the effect is just "right."

WordPerfect 5.0's graphics handling ability is matched by its strong document organizing features and its control over typography. You can easily compile a table of contents, an index, as well as lists of imported graphics and text files. You can edit a text file with the knowledge that imported graphics files (and their captions) will remain adjacent to the text to which they relate. You can include numerous typefaces on a page. You can adjust line and letter spacing to tolerances close enough to please the most exacting art director or typesetter.

Once created, WordPerfect 5.0 PostScript files can be set in type on such high-resolution output devices as the Linotronic 100 or 300. Phototypesetting at 1270 or 2540 dots per inch, instead of the 300 dots per inch offered by laser printing, allows documents such as this book to rival the quality of yesterday's best composition methods.

This isn't to say that WordPerfect 5.0 should be the only software program you'll ever use. Design-intensive projects (e.g., logos, posters or single-page image advertisements) may require the use of outside drawing programs, such as Arts & Letters, Micrografix Designer and PC Paintbrush—all of which are excellent partners for WordPerfect 5.0.

WordPerfect 5.0 versus Dedicated Page Layout Programs

At what point should you consider moving beyond WordPerfect and investigate a dedicated page layout program? The answer depends upon both the design sophistication of your project and the point at which the added productivity of a dedicated page layout program makes the purchase of the program economically feasible.

The type of work you do should be a major deciding factor. If you're a designer who spends a lot of time creating one-of-a-kind projects like logos, posters or single-page advertisements, you may find that the continuous WYSIWYG (What-You-See-Is-What-You-Get) screen display of a dedicated page layout program is worth the added expense.

If you're like most people, however, your work probably involves a combination of writing, formatting and text organization. During the course of a week, you probably work on many types of multi-page documents, including brochures, newsletters, proposals, price lists and other projects. For you, WordPerfect 5.0 probably offers all the desktop publishing power you need. It lets you format your words and enhance them with imported graphics, without having to leave WordPerfect and load another program.

The Dangerous Job of Attempting to Predict the Future

It's also important to recognize that WordPerfect 5.0 is probably just the first in a series of enhanced versions that will increase the desktop publishing power of WordPerfect's basic word processing "engine." The differences between WordPerfect and dedicated page layout programs will become fewer and fewer with each new WordPerfect release.

Possible enhancements may include improved on-screen display, on-screen rulers and a more interactive **VIEW DOCU-MENT** mode, which would allow you to edit while viewing all, or magnified portions, of a single page or two-page spread.

Future versions probably will allow you to create oversized documents and will expand WordPerfect's color-handling capabilities. As a new generation of color laser printers begins to appear, WordPerfect undoubtedly will keep pace by allowing you to "mix" colors on-screen and prepare spot-color overlays or even four-color separations.

As image-scanners grow in popularity, WordPerfect perhaps will add a capability that lets you modify the contrast range of scanned photographs so they'll reproduce best on the type of paper you use to print your project.

All of the above should be classified as "conjecture" rather than as authorized "predictions." They're included here to emphasize that as your desktop publishing needs become more sophisticated, WordPerfect will grow right along with you. The above enhancements, in short, are simply based on common sense and WordPerfect's proven tradition of "listening to the market."

So, jump on the WordPerfect desktop publishing bandwagon. WordPerfect 5.0 and versions that follow promise to have a profound impact on the appearance of printed documents of all types. Desktop publishing has never been easier or more affordable. By becoming familiar with WordPerfect 5.0's desktop publishing capabilities now, you can easily keep up with the program as its powers become stronger and stronger.

Appendix

The following is a list of just a few of the hardware and software enhancements that can help you get the most out of *Desktop Publishing with WordPerfect 5.0*.

Adobe Systems, Inc., P.O. Box 7900, Mountain View, CA 94039-7900. 415-961-4400

Adobe publishes one of the largest collections of downloadable fonts for PostScript printers, such as the Apple LaserWriter IINT, as well as the Linotronic 100 and 300 phototypesetters. Most Adobe fonts are licensed by the International Typographic Corporation (ITC), which ensures quality and compatibility with typefaces available from conventional phototypesetters.

Adobe publishes the *Typeface Catalog* ($15), which contains illustrations of character sets for all of its typefaces, as well as samples of typical applications for each particular typeface.

Adobe's Publisher's Packages should be of interest to those who're taking their first steps beyond resident fonts. These specially priced packages consist of two, or more, typeface families that work well together and are appropriate for particular categories of projects.

For example, Adobe's "Package Number One: Newsletters" consists of two serif and one sans serif typefaces that can add a distinct appearance to your newsletter.

Bitstream, Inc., Athenaeum House, 215 First Street, Cambridge, MA 02142. 617-497-6222

Bitstream produces digital type of ITC quality for users of both PostScript and HP-compatible printers. Bitstream also has designed several typefaces, created to work particularly well in a variety of sizes with laser-output devices. More than one hundred typefaces are available, with more being added each month.

Because Bitstream font outlines can be used with either family of laser printers, your investment is preserved if you change from an HP-compatible to a PostScript printer.

Bitstream publishes a free catalog showing sample alphabet sets from its wide selection of typefaces.

Computer Support Corporation, 15926 Midway Road, Dallas, TX 75244. 214-661-8960

Arts & Letters is a combination of a Microsoft Windows-based drawing program and a clip art library consisting of 1,100 sample symbols and drawings. These can be combined in various ways, stored in a variety of formats, including Encapsulated PostScript file and placed in a WordPerfect 5.0 document.

Hercules Computer Technology, Inc., 921 Parker Street, Berkeley, CA 94710. 415-540-6000

Hercules manufactures several graphics cards, including a black and white version, a network version and the In-Color RamFont Card. These cards and accompanying software expedite page layout and formatting by giving you an on-screen representation of increased or decreased type size, as well as such attributes as boldface, italics, underlining and boldface italicized type.

The Hercules RamFont cards should be of special interest to those preparing long documents, designed to use a few type sizes and type styles consistently.

Micrografx, 1820 N. Greenville Avenue, Richardson, TX 75801. 214-234-1769

Micrografx Designer is a sophisticated Windows-based drawing program that can be used to create sophisticated logos and drawings for placement in WordPerfect 5.0 documents.

PC Publishing, 950 Lee Street, Des Plaines, IL 60016. 312-296-0770

Personal Publishing, 25W550 Geneva Road, Wheaton, IL 60188. 312-665-1000

Publish! 501 Second Street, San Francisco, CA 94107. 415-243-0600

These three publications are "must" reading for anyone who wants to keep abreast of the rapidly changing field of desktop publishing. You'll learn the latest tips and techniques, plus stay up-to-date on new hardware and software offerings.

Choosing between them is a matter of personal preference. *PC Publishing* gains its strength from its emphasis upon MS-DOS desktop publishing.

Personal Publishing and *Publish!* differ in personality, but both include developments in both Apple Macintosh and MS-DOS-based desktop publishing.

QMS, One Magnus Pass, Mobile, AL 36618. 205-633-4300

The QMS JetScript is a hardware/software upgrade which lets Hewlett-Packard LaserJet Series II owners add PostScript capability to their printer. The QMS JetScript consists of two printed circuit boards (one of which is added to your printer and the other to your computer) plus appropriate software.

The primary advantage of the QMS JetScript is that it allows LaserJet Series II owners to make laser proofs of documents that will later be phototypeset on a Linotronic 100 or 300. Installation doesn't void Hewlett-Packard's warranty and, once installed, the LaserJet can be used as either a Hewlett-Packard PCL printer or a PostScript printer.

Softcraft, Inc., 16 North Carroll Street, Suite 500, Madison, WI 53703. 608-257-3300

Softcraft publishes several programs which, when used in conjunction with Bitstream's bit-mapped fonts, make many PostScript features accessible to users of HP-compatible printers.

Softcraft's Font Effects program, for example, lets you add special effects like shadows, outlines, striped interiors, shaded backgrounds and other special effects. You also can slant, enlarge, reduce, embolden or lighten a font—creative powers that were previously unavailable on HP-compatible printers.

The Softcraft Font Editor allows you to create your own typefaces, for special purposes like logos or headline effects.

Symsoft, Inc., 444 First Street, Suite K, Los Altos, CA 94022. 415-941-1552

Symsoft's HotShot Plus and HotShot Graphics are two utility programs that will be of special interest to those who're using WordPerfect 5.0 to create computer or software documentation.

HotShot Plus is a memory-resident screen capture program that can save any text or graphics appearing on the screen of your computer to a file that can be placed in a WordPerfect document. HotShot Graphics is an editing program that lets you modify screen capture images and organize them into easily accessed "picture databases."

T/Maker Company, 1973 Landings Drive, Mountain View, CA 94043. 415-962-0195

T/Maker publishes several packages of ClickArt—pre-drawn illustrations which can be easily imported to newsletters or other projects. One of its most useful packages is the Business Images package which includes more than 1,000 industrial and business symbols and borders, including drawings of office equipment and supplies.

T/Maker's newest addition is a series of high-quality EPS illustrations, which consist of high-quality Encapsulated PostScript File images. Because they can be increased or decreased in size without resulting in a loss of quality, the utility of these images is extremely high. Included are country /state maps, as well as frequently used symbols such as credit cards, male/female symbols and drawings with seasonal themes. An illustrated index helps you quickly locate any desired image.

Ventana Press, P.O. Box 2468, Chapel Hill, NC 27515.   919-942-0220

Looking Good in Print: A Guide to Basic Design for Desktop Publishing, by Roger C. Parker, is a generic guide to creating professional-looking, easy-to-read publications. Section One describes the basic elements of effective design. Section Two includes several "before" and "after" makeover samples. Section Three addresses design considerations for specific project categories, including advertisements, brochures and newsletters.

The WordPerfect Support Group, P.O. Box 1577, Baltimore, MD 21203
800-USA-GROUP
800-872-4768
301-889-7893

The world's largest independent group of WordPerfect users, with more than 28,000 members worldwide. Through *The WordPerfectionist* (an informative monthly newsletter) and CompuServe Forum, users become more knowledgeable through shared experience.

Index

From the Ventana Press Desktop Design Series:

If you're serious about making your printed materials look their best, *Looking Good in Print* by Roger C. Parker, shows you how to put proven design techniques to work on your computer--quickly and economically.

Looking Good in Print helps you create appealing, persuasive printed materials, with simple, down-to-earth solutions for nearly any design project.

> "The writing is clear and to the point. For either those who are starting out with desktop publishing or those who have been working with it for a while and want to improve their designs, *Looking Good in Print* is an excellent and valuable resource."
> --*PC Week*

> "Parker's book is a valuable addition to the library of any publisher--desktop or not."
> --*Publish!* Magazine

Available in bookstores or from Ventana Press. Your money returned in full if not satisfied.

Softcover, 7-⅜" x 9-¼"
220 pages, illustrated
ISBN: 0-940087-05-7
$23.95

———— Yes, please send ———— copies of **Looking Good in Print,** at $23.95/book. Add $2.40 for normal shipping, $5.00 for UPS "two-day air." NC residents add 5% sales tax. Money returned in full if not satisfied.

Name ————————————————————— Firm —————————————————————

Address (no P.O. Box) ——————————————————————————————————

City ——————————————————— State ———————————— Zip ————————————

Telephone ————————————————

———————— Payment enclosed (check or money order; no cash please)

VISA Acc't # ——————————————————— MC Acc't # ————————————————————

Exp. Date ———————————— Signature —————————————————————————

MAIL TO: Ventana Press   P.O. Box 2468   Chapel Hill, NC 27515   919/942-0220

Please send me _____ additional copies of *Desktop Publishing with Word-Perfect* at $21.95 per book. Add $2.40 a book for normal UPS shipping; $5 for two-day air. NC residents add 5% sales tax. Immediate shipment guaranteed.

Note: 15% discount for purchases of 5-9 books. 20% discount for purchases of 10 or more books. Resellers please call for wholesale discount information.

Name: _____ Firm: _____

Address (no P.O. box): _____

City: _____ State: _____ Zip: _____

Telephone: _____

_____ Check or money order enclosed.

Visa or MC Account #: _____

Exp. Date: _____ Signature: _____

Ventana Press ■ Post Office Box 2468 ■ Chapel Hill, NC 27515 ■ 919/942-0220

Please send me _____ additional copies of *Desktop Publishing with Word-Perfect* at $21.95 per book. Add $2.40 a book for normal UPS shipping; $5 for two-day air. NC residents add 5% sales tax. Immediate shipment guaranteed.

Note: 15% discount for purchases of 5-9 books. 20% discount for purchases of 10 or more books. Resellers please call for wholesale discount information.

Name: _____ Firm: _____

Address (no P.O. box): _____

City: _____ State: _____ Zip: _____

Telephone: _____

_____ Check or money order enclosed.

Visa or MC Account #: _____

Exp. Date: _____ Signature: _____

Ventana Press ■ Post Office Box 2468 ■ Chapel Hill, NC 27515 ■ 919/942-0220

NO POSTAGE
NECESSARY
IF MAILED
IN THE
UNITED STATES

BUSINESS REPLY MAIL

FIRST CLASS MAIL   PERMIT #495   CHAPEL HILL, NC

POSTAGE WILL BE PAID BY ADDRESSEE

Ventana Press

P.O. Box 2468

Chapel Hill, NC 27515

NO POSTAGE
NECESSARY
IF MAILED
IN THE
UNITED STATES

BUSINESS REPLY MAIL

FIRST CLASS MAIL   PERMIT #495   CHAPEL HILL, NC

POSTAGE WILL BE PAID BY ADDRESSEE

Ventana Press

P.O. Box 2468

Chapel Hill, NC 27515